A MODERN GUIDE TO INDULGENCES

Rediscovering This Often Misinterpreted Teaching

Edward N. Peters, JD, J

HillenbrandBooks

Chicago / Mundelein, Illinois

Nihil Obstat
Reverend William H. Woestman, OMI, JCD
Censor Deputatus
March 7, 2008

Imprimatur
Reverend John F. Canary, STL, DMIN
Vicar General
Archdiocese of Chicago
March 14, 2008

A MODERN GUIDE TO INDULGENCES © 2008 Archdiocese of Chicago: Liturgy Training Publications, 3949 South Racine Avenue, Chicago IL 60609; 1-800-933-1800, fax 1-800-933-7094, e-mail orders@ltp.org. All rights reserved. See our Web site at www.LTP.org.

Hillenbrand Books is an imprint of Liturgy Training Publications (LTP) and the Liturgical Institute at the University of Saint Mary of the Lake (USML). The imprint is focused on contemporary and classical theological thought concerning the liturgy of the Catholic Church. Available at bookstores everywhere, or through LTP by calling 1-800-933-1800 or visiting www.LTP.org. Further information about the **Hillenbrand Books** publishing program is available from the University of Saint Mary of the Lake/Mundelein Seminary, 1000 East Maple Avenue, Mundelein, IL 60060 (847-837-4542), on the Web at www.usml.edu/liturgicalinstitute, or e-mail litinst@usml.edu.

Cover © The Crosiers/Gene Plaisted, osc

Printed in the United States of America.

Library of Congress Cataloging-in-Publication Data 2008923892

13 12 11 10   6 5 4 3 2

ISBN 978-1-59525-024-7

HMGI

For
Thomas, Charles, Catherine, Robert, Margaret, Theresa, Mary, Theresa, Michael, Khun, Luisa, and Krishna.

Contents

Preface

It has been nearly five hundred years since Martin Luther nailed his
Ninety-five Theses to the cathedral door in Wittenberg, targeting
chiefly, in those early days of religious revolution, the Catholic Church's
doctrine on indulgences. With roots deep in the ancient Church,
indulgences had by Luther's time been part of Christian life for more
than a thousand years, but by the sixteenth century, they were admittedly in need of significant re-explanation and re-regulation. But such
was the fury hurled at indulgences that even today, five centuries later,
although Church teaching on indulgences has never been clearer and
abuses in practice so entirely rooted out, they still go largely ignored.[1]
This short book aims to correct that situation.

Any Christian—for most indulgences are available not just to
Catholics, but to all the baptized—can obtain indulgences for personal benefit, for the welfare of the Christian community (in particular
of the dead), and most importantly, for the greater glory of God. To
further those ends, I will first present explanations of the Church's
doctrine of indulgences, and second, offer descriptions of and brief
commentary on the major indulgences currently in force. Because
indulgences are, as we shall see, closely linked to the pastoral application
of Church teaching on sin, reconciliation, and sacramental Confession,
I will discuss these important concepts in relation to the gift of
indulgences within the faith and life of modern Christians.

In general, I have tried to maintain a more popular tone in
the main text of this book, while reserving for the footnotes more
detailed explanations and references for further study. The *Catechism
of the Catholic Church* and the *1983 Code of Canon Law* are also useful

---

1. Sometimes indulgences are more than just ignored. As recently as 1999, the strong
antipathy against indulgences still felt by some non-Catholic Christian leaders was seen when,
in response to the announcement by Pope John Paul II that he was going to declare a special
indulgence for the Millennial Jubilee celebration (see John Paul II, Bull of Indiction, *Incarnationis
Mysterium*, 29 November 1998), the World Alliance of Reformed Churches withdrew in protest its fraternal delegate to the Catholic Church's Central Committee for the Great Jubilee of
2000. See P. Palmer and G. Tavard, "Indulgences," *New Catholic Encyclopedia*, 2d ed.
(Thomson-Gale, 2003) vol. 7, pp. 436–441, at 440.

for understanding indulgences and are so widely available today that I have included most of the references to those two works directly in the text.

As they have done so often, the Rev. Joseph Koterski, sj, stl, phd, and Mark Brumley, mts, placed me ever deeper in their debt by making many helpful comments on earlier drafts of this work. Would that I could repay half the kindnesses these gentlemen have shown me over the years.

I am also most grateful to Dr. Robert Fastiggi, who kindly provided a historical introduction that helps place the entire work in context.

Foreword

"Hallelujah! Give thanks to the LORD, who is good, whose love endures forever." (Psalm 106)

I can well remember my course in the "Introduction to the Old Testament" at the Angelicum University in Rome. The renowned Biblical scholar, Peter Paul Zerafa, OP, told us that the characteristic most attributed to the Lord in the Hebrew Scriptures was *mercy*. Then I think of the prayers that most touched the Sacred Heart of Jesus: always succinct, sincere, simple, such as "Jesus, Son of David, have *mercy* on me!"

Fast forward to now, to a devotion, relatively new, which has captivated the world: *Divine Mercy.* You get the point: God is rich in mercy, and his people can never fail to move him by asking for it.

In all the commentary surrounding the passing of Pope John Paul II, I found it touching that the only office of the Vatican whose duties did not cease at the death of a Pontiff was that of the Apostolic Penitentiary, that organ of the Holy See responsible for assuring God's people of *mercy* in unusually complicated and delicate situations. Yes, "His *mercy* endures forever!" The Lord—and his Church—will go to any end to display and dispense the overwhelming lavish *mercy* promised us.

Bring on *indulgences*, a beautiful, tender, powerful, tangible sign of God's potent *mercy.* Unfortunately, because they are often misunderstood, this classic component of the Church's arsenal against sin has been ridiculed and forgotten the last four decades.

That's why we can welcome this fascinating, comprehensive, scholarly-yet-readable study by Dr. Edward Peters on *indulgences.* His research into Scripture, the Fathers, the towering theologians of our tradition, Church doctrine, the Councils, and the Magisterium of the Church is impressive, giving us not only a renewed appreciation for the topic of *indulgences*, but a deeper knowledge of sin, grace, redemption, the merits of Christ, and the very nature of the Church.

I don't know about you, but I need all the help I can get in improving my prayer and better comprehending the explosive power of God's *mercy*. Dr. Peters supplies such help. I think this book is good enough to have an indulgence attached to reading it!

Most Reverend Timothy M. Dolan
Archbishop of New York

Introduction

A Short History and Theology of Indulgences

The word indulgence comes from Latin word *indulgentia*, which means a show of kindness or tenderness. The verbal root is *indulgere*: to forgive, to be lenient toward or be tender toward. The Catholic theology of indulgences is closely connected with the sacrament of penance, which is why the treatment of indulgences follows that of penance in both the 1983 *Code of Canon Law* (canons 992–997) and the *Catechism of the Catholic Church* (paragraphs 1471–1479). Indulgences likewise are linked to Catholic soteriology, which understands justification as not merely the forgiveness of sins but also "the sanctification and renewal of the interior man."[1]

The process of sanctification and interior renewal requires not only forgiveness from the guilt (*culpa*) of sin but also purification from the harmful effects or wounds of sin. The call of Christ to "be perfect, just as your heavenly Father is perfect" (Matthew 5:48) is ultimately a call for interior purification. Spiritual writers describe this as the mystical path of purgation, illumination, and union with God. This spiritual path has an eschatological dimension, for it culminates in the beatific vision and the communion of saints. This is why Catholics believe in Purgatory or post-mortem purification. People die in the state of grace or friendship with God, but the effects of sin on the soul often remain. Since "nothing unclean" can enter heaven (cf. Revelation 21:27), the souls of the deceased can still carry harmful effects of sin and must, therefore, be purified before entering the fullness of the heavenly kingdom.

---

1. The Council of Trent, *Decree on Justification* [AD 1547]: Denzinger- Hünermann, *Enchiridion symbolorum definitionum et declarationum de rebus fidei et morum* 40th ed. (Freiburg: Herder, 2005) [Denz-H], no.1528.

1

The path to purification is never solitary. We rely upon the support of others within the Church to assist us by their prayers and offerings. Through the sacraments, especially the Eucharist, we link ourselves to the communion of the faithful: those on earth, those undergoing post-mortem purification and those in heaven "beholding 'clearly God Himself, one and Triune, exactly as He is.' "[2] As Vatican II teaches, there is a "communication of spiritual goods" that links the faithful on earth with the souls in purgatory and the saints in heaven.[3]

The Catholic doctrine of indulgences, therefore, cannot be understood without appreciating its intimate connection with Catholic doctrines related to sin, justification, penance, purification, Purgatory, and the communion of saints. It is not surprising that the Protestant conception of justification led to not only the rejection of indulgences but also to the eventual abandonment of the sacrament of penance, prayers for the departed, and belief in Purgatory. All of these doctrines are so intimately linked that when one is rejected, the others likewise fade away.

The *Catechism of the Catholic Church* defines an indulgence as:

> . . . a remission before God of the temporal punishment due to sins whose guilt has already been forgiven, which the faithful Christian who is duly disposed gains under certain prescribed conditions through the action of the Church which, as the minister of redemption, dispenses and applies with authority the treasury of the satisfactions of Christ and the saints.[4]

THEOLOGICAL BASIS OF INDULGENCES

Behind this definition are a number of theological terms that need further explanation. The first is temporal punishment due to sin. The Catholic Church recognizes that sin has "a double consequence."[5] Unrepentant grave sins, committed with full knowledge and deliberate consent,[6] deprive a person of eternal life with God (cf. 1 Corinthians

---

2. Vatican II, *Lumen gentium*, 49.

3. Ibid.

4. Catechism of the Catholic Church [CCC], 1471; cf. also Pope Paul VI, apostolic constitution, *Indulgentiarum doctrina* [1967], Norm 1.

5. CCC, 1472.

6. Cf. CCC, 1857.

6:9–10; Galatians 5:21; Revelation 21:8). But all sins, even those that are not deadly (cf. 1 John 5:17), still involve "an unhealthy attachment to creatures, which must be purified either here on earth, or after death in the state called Purgatory."[7]

The temporal punishment due to sin is, as the name suggests, time bound and not eternal. It is not a penalty imposed from without but something that follows "from the very nature of sin."[8] Sin affects not only our relationship with God, but it also injures our character and damages our relations with others. The translator of Dante, Dorothy Sayers, gives an example of someone who, in a fit of rage or carelessness, destroys a valuable vase of a friend. When the person apologizes and the friend forgives, the guilt or *culpa* of the destructive act is taken away. There remains, however, the need "to purge the *reatus*" or fault which led to the breaking of the vase in the first place.[9] Moreover, there is the need to make reparation for the damaged vase itself.

Human experience confirms what the Catholic Church teaches about the reality of sin. There are temporal effects that follow from the very nature of sin itself. This is why the sacrament of penance involves not only sorrow or contrition but also confession and satisfaction. Not all the disorders caused by sin are taken away by sacramental absolution.[10] As the *Catechism* teaches: "Raised up from sin, the sinner must still recover his full spiritual health by doing something more to make amends for the sin: he must 'make satisfaction for' or 'expiate' his sins."[11] This is what the Church calls penance or satisfaction, which can involve prayers, sacrifices, or acts of service that seek to heal the temporal effects of sin: those injuries inflicted by the sin on both the sinner and others.

In addition to the concept of the temporal punishment due to sin, the Catholic definition of indulgence also involves the notion of the Church as "the minister of redemption." This is a concept that most Protestants resist because of their tendency to understand the Church

---

7. Ibid.

8. Ibid.

9. Dante, *The Divine Comedy 2: Purgatory* trans. Dorothy L. Sayers, (London: Penguin Books, 1955): Introduction, 48.

10. Cf. CCC, 1459.

11. Ibid.

as "the congregation of the elect" rather than the Body of Christ. Catholics, though, understand the Church as a visible, sacramental reality through which Christ "communicated grace and truth to all."[12] The visible Church, with her "hierarchical organs" can be compared to the human nature of the Incarnate Word, which serves as "a living organ of salvation."[13] Christ communicates grace through his Body, the Church, and he gives to his apostles and their successors the power to bind and loose (Matthew 18:18) and the power to forgive sins in his name (John 20:23).

By means of this sacramental mediation, the Church serves as "the minister of redemption" to the faithful, especially through Baptism, the Eucharist, and the Sacrament of Penance. In addition to the sacramental mediation of grace, the Church, by virtue of the keys entrusted to Peter and his successors (cf. Matthew 16:19), draws upon the "treasure" of the infinite merits of Christ and the immense merits of the Blessed Virgin Mary and the saints. These merits can be distributed to the faithful for their spiritual benefit in the form of indulgences or grants of tenderness, which help to purify the faithful from the temporal effects of sin.

Only in the context of the penitential life of the Church can indulgences be properly understood. Although the practice of indulgences only developed concretely in the eleventh century, the theological basis for them is found in both scripture and the penitential life of the early Church.

A Brief History of Indulgences

Scripture very clearly testifies to the link between sin and temporal punishments. After the fall of Adam and Eve, the woman is told that her pain in childbirth will be intensified (Genesis 3:16), and the man is informed that he will labor for bread by the sweat of his face (Genesis 3:19). Even after God forgives David for his sin of adultery, there is the further punishment of the death of the child conceived and born from the sin (2 Samuel 12:13–14).

12. Vatican II, *Lumen gentium*, 8.
13. Ibid.

In the Bible, we see the power of prayer and offerings on behalf of others. In 2 Maccabees 12:42–46, a collection is taken up for an expiatory sacrifice to make atonement for the sins of the Jewish soldiers who had died wearing amulets of the gods of Jamnia. Scripture also teaches that we can link our sufferings to those of Christ "on behalf of His body, which is the Church" (cf. Colossians 1:24). Moreover, our prayers can help lead others to repentance (cf. 1 John 5:16) and contribute to the forgiveness of their sins (cf. James 5:15). In the New Testament, there is likewise evidence of the Church imposing penances. Saint Paul, for example, urges forgiveness for an offender who has endured the punishment he received (2 Corinthians 2:5–10).

In the early Church, public penances were often required of those who had committed grievous sins like apostasy. Reconciliation with the Church was a communal affair, and early Christian writers like Tertullian (c. 150–220) recognized that "the whole body must suffer and work together for a cure" when some members are sick.[14] Along these lines, public penitents would sometimes obtain from those to be martyred a *libellus* (petition or letter) stating that the martyr would offer his or her sufferings on behalf of the penitent. Both Tertullian and Cyprian of Carthage (c. 200–258) testify to the acceptance of these *libelli* as grounds for shortening required times of penance.[15]

Even if the term *indulgentia* was not used for these grants of mercy, similar terms such as *remissio* were. *Indulgentia* was a term used in Roman civil law for the grant of a right, privilege, or pardon.[16] Early Christian rulers also used the term in this sense. The Council of Toledo of 633, however, used the term *indulgentia* for the ceremony reconciling penitents on Good Friday.[17]

As penitential practices developed from the sixth to the tenth centuries, there was a gradual move from public to private penances. Handbooks of penances known as the *Poenitentiales,* which stipulated very specific penances for certain types of sins, were utilized by confessors. Various bishops, however, would often allow for the substitution

---

14. Tertullian, *De Paenitentia* 10:5.

15. Cf. Alexius M. Lépicier, osm, *Indulgences: Their Origin, Nature and Development* (London: Kegan Paul, Trench and Tübner, 1906), 202–213.

16. Rev. Joseph Edward Campbell, *Indulgences: The Ordinary Power of Prelates Inferior to the Pope to Grant Indulgences* (Ottawa: The University of Ottawa Press, 1953), 53.

17. Ibid.

of certain prayers (e.g., the Psalms), fasts, and almsgiving in place of the standard penances (which were often quite demanding). By the ninth century, popes and bishops "frequently concluded their letters with a petition (*suffragium*) asking God through the intercession of Christ and the saints to absolve the sinner of all remaining penalties due to sin."[18]

By the eleventh century, the practice of granting indulgences became more pronounced. Indulgences were granted for the construction or support of "churches, schools, hospitals and bridges."[19] Indulgences were linked to various places of pilgrimage such as Santiago de Compostela in Spain. Pope Urban II, at the Council of Clermont in 1095, offered a plenary indulgence that decreed: "Whoever out of pure devotion and not for the purpose of gaining honor or money shall go to Jerusalem to liberate the Church of God, let that journey be counted in lieu of all penance."[20]

By the thirteenth century, indulgences were well established in the life of Catholic Europe. Since indulgences were sometimes prone to abuse, the Fourth Lateran Council (1215) warned about "indiscriminate and excessive indulgences" (*indiscretas et superfluas indulgentias*), and ruled that when a new basilica is dedicated "the indulgence shall not be for more than one year."[21]

Medieval theologians such as Hugh of Saint-Cher (c. 1200–1263), Bonaventure (c. 1217–1274) and Thomas Aquinas (c. 1225–1274) discussed the nature and application of indulgences. Hugh linked indulgences to the Church as the Mystical Body of Christ. Bonaventure understood indulgences in terms of vicarious satisfaction for the sins of others. Aquinas recognized that "the plenitude of power for granting indulgences resides in the Pope,"[22] but bishops, subject to the Pope's regulation, can grant indulgences "within fixed limits and not

---

18. P.F. Palmer and G.A. Tavard, "Indulgences" in *New Catholic Encyclopedia* Second Edition (Detroit: Thomson Gale, 2003), Vol. 7, 346.

19. Ibid.

20. W.H. Kent, "Indulgences," in *Catholic Encyclopedia* (New York: The Encyclopedia Press, 1913), vol. VII, 786.

21. Norman Tanner, sj, ed. *Decrees of the Ecumenical Councils*, Vol. I (London and Washington, D.C.: Sheed & Ward and Georgetown University Press, 1990), 263–264.

22. Thomas Aquinas, *Summa theologica*, trans. Fathers of the English Dominican Province (Allen, TX: Christian Classics, 1981) supplement, q. 26, art. 3

beyond."[23] Saint Thomas also believed that even priests and deacons
could grant indulgences by means of delegated jurisdiction.[24]

In the year 1300, Pope Boniface VIII promulgated a special
indulgence for pilgrims coming to Rome for the Jubilee year, thereby
setting a precedent for subsequent Jubilee years, including 2000 AD.
Pope Clement VI (r. 1342–1352) decided that Jubilee indulgences
should be granted every 50 rather than 100 years. In 1343, he issued
the bull, *Unigenitus Dei Filius*, in anticipation of the Jubilee year, 1350.
In this document, he articulates a theology of indulgences based on
the treasury of merits (of Christ, the Blessed Virgin Mary and the
saints) entrusted to the Church via the keys to the kingdom of heaven
(given to Saint Peter and his successors).[25] The basic points of Clement
VI's bull became normative for Catholic theology for centuries.

Pope Martin V, in his bull, *Inter cunctas*, of February 22, 1418,
presented a list of questions for the followers of Wyclif and Hus.
Among these are two that pertain to indulgences.[26] Basically, Martin
V wanted to know whether these followers acknowledged the authority of the Pope to grant indulgences "for a pious and just cause,"
especially to those who make pilgrimages and visit churches.

The issue of indulgences assumed prominence in the controversies surrounding Martin Luther (1483–1546). In his Ninety-five
Theses made public in October, 1517, Luther seemed to accept the
apostolic origin of indulgences (thesis 71), but he questioned the
power of the Pope to remit guilt "save by declaring and confirming
what has been remitted by God" (thesis 6). Furthermore, he appeared
to deny the power of the Pope to grant plenary indulgences except
with regard to penalties imposed by the Pope himself (thesis 20).[27]

In late May of 1518, Luther sent a copy of a treatise explaining his theses to Pope Leo X. He told the Pontiff that he would defer
to his judgment, saying: "I shall recognize your words as the words of
Christ speaking in you."[28] From October 12–14, 1518, Luther met

---

23. Ibid.

24. Ibid. q. 26, art. 2.

25. Cf. Denz.-H, 1025–1027.

26. Cf. Ibid., 1266–1267.

27. Cf. Bettenson, Henry and Maunder, Chris, eds., *Documents of the Christian Church*
Third Edition (Oxford: Oxford University Press, 1999), 206–212.

28. Preserved Smith, *The Life and Letters of Martin Luther* (Boston: Houghton Mifflin
Company, 1911), 45

with Cardinal Cajetan, the papal delegate, to discuss his theology. By this time, Luther was raising more serious doubts about the Catholic theology of indulgences. He questioned the authority of Clement VI's 1343 bull, *Unigenitus Dei Filius.* Cajetan tried unsuccessfully to have Luther recant some of his positions. The case was referred back to the Pope, and on Novembert 9, 1518, the papal decree, *Cum postquam,* was issued by Leo X.[29] This decree reaffirmed Catholic teaching on indulgences, along the lines of *Unigenitus Dei Filius.*

Luther did not accept the teaching of Pope Leo X as he said he would. Instead, his rhetoric grew more radical. On June 15, 1520, the papal bull, *Exsurge Domine,* was issued, censuring 41 propositions of Luther. Among the censured propositions was one stating that: "Indulgences are a pious fraud on the faithful dispensing them from doing good works" (18), and another saying: "They are led astray who believe that indulgences are salutary and spiritually fruitful" (20).[30] Furthermore, Luther was censured for denying that indulgences are useful for "the dead and the dying."[31]

Luther was excommunicated in 1521, and he died in 1546. The Council of Trent did not take up the question of indulgences until its twenty-fifth session in 1563. The Council reaffirmed indulgences as "most salutary to the Christian people" and ordered that their use be retained by the Church.[32] Moreover, it condemned under anathema those who deny the power of the Church to grant them. The Council did, however, demand that any trafficking in indulgences for monetary gain be absolutely abolished lest the good name of indulgences "be blasphemed by the heretics."[33] In 1597, Pope Pius V abolished all indulgences that required fees or payment.

The theologians of the post-Tridentine period, such as the Jesuit Francisco Suárez (1548–1617), defended the practice of indulgences. In 1669, the oversight of indulgences was delegated to the newly created Congregation for Indulgences and Relics. This Congregation became responsible for the various editions of the *Raccolta* (collection) of Indulgences that appeared in 1807, 1877, 1886, and 1898. This

---

29. Cf. Denz.-H, 1447–1449.
30. Cf. Ibid., 1468 and 1470.
31. Ibid., 1472.
32. Denz.-H., 1835.
33. Ibid.

Congregation also regulated indulgences attached to special altars called "privileged altars." In 1840, it ruled that the efficacy of indulgences attached to such altars ultimately "corresponds to the good will and favor of the divine mercy"—even if a plenary indulgence is intended.[34]

In 1908, Pope Pius X abolished the Congregation for Indulgences and Relics and transferred the oversight of indulgences to the Holy Office. In 1935, Pope Benedict XV removed the section on indulgences from the Holy Office and joined it to the Apostolic Penitentiary. New editions of the *Raccolta* continued to be issued periodically. In 1988, the apostolic constitution *Pastor Bonus* reaffirmed the competence of the Apostolic Penitentiary over indulgences, except in cases when the Congregation for the Doctrine of the Faith needs to examine doctrinal questions related to them.

Without doubt, the most significant document on indulgences since the Council of Trent was the 1967 apostolic constitution, *Indulgentiarum doctrina*, of Paul VI. This document provides a firm scriptural, historical, and spiritual foundation for the Catholic theology of indulgences. Among its most significant reforms is the abolition of all references to "days" or "years." Instead, indulgences are divided into two categories, plenary and partial, depending on whether they free a person from "either part or all of the temporal punishment due to sin." (norm n. 2).[35] Paul VI specifies that in addition to the standard requirements for gaining a plenary indulgence (the performance of the indulgenced work, sacramental confession, eucharistic communion and prayers for the pope's intentions), there is the further requirement that "all attachment to sin, even venial sin, be absent."[36] This requirement underscores the ultimate purpose of indulgences: the purification of the soul from all effects of sin.

Paul VI also makes it clear that the treasury of the Church "should certainly not be imagined as the sum total of the material goods accumulated in the course of centuries."[37] Ultimately, "the treasury of the Church . . . is Christ the Redeemer himself in whom

---

34. Denz.-H, 2750.

35. Translation taken from the Vatican Web site: http://www.vatican.va/holy_father/paul_vi/apost_constitutions/documents/hf_p-vi_apc_19670101_indulgen (accessed 5/16/2007).

36. Paul VI, *Indulgentiarum doctrina*, norm 7.

37. Ibid., II, no. 5.

the satisfaction and merit of his redemption exist and find their force."[38]
The "prayers and good works of the Blessed Virgin Mary and all the
saints" are added to "the truly immense, unfathomable and ever pristine
value" of Christ's saving work because "they have also cooperated in
the salvation of their brothers in the unity of the Mystical Body."[39]

Paul VI's constitution provided the basis for the presentation
of indulgences both in the 1983 *Code of Canon Law* and the 1992/1997
Catechism of the Catholic Church. In 1999, Pope John Paul II issued
Incarnationis mysterium, the bull of indiction for the Jubilee year, 2000.
In this document, the norms for gaining indulgences for the Jubilee
were specified, and the Holy Father highlighted the special theme of
pilgrimages as "an exercise of practical asceticism, repentance and
conversion."[40] In 1999, the Apostolic Penitentiary also issued an
updated version of the *Enchiridion indulgentiarum: Normae et concessiones*
[Handbook of Indulgences: Norms and Grants]. Dr. Peters beauti-
fully present the details of this Enchiridion in the present text.

Indulgences are offered to the faithful as resources of purgation
and sanctification.[41] Moreover, the faithful are able to apply their
indulgences to the souls in Purgatory "as suffrages."[42] These suffrages
are intercessions or appeals to God for the purification of souls in
Purgatory. Like all prayers and offerings for others, indulgences applied
to the dead ultimately depend upon the good will of God and his
mercy. We cannot control how they apply by our own efforts. The
Church, though, recognizes that "the faithful who offer indulgences in
suffrage for the dead . . . cultivate charity in an excellent way and
while raising their minds to heaven they bring a wiser order into the
things of this world."[43] Just as our prayers and offerings can help the
living be detached from their sins,[44] so indulgences can be offered to
the dead as suffrages (supports or intercessions) to help them in their
final process of purification.

---

38. Ibid.

39. Ibid.

40. *John* Paul II, *Incarnationis mysterium* [1999], no. 7. The Bull was approved on Nov. 29,
1998, but issued publicly in 1999.

41. Paul VI, *Indulgentiarum doctrina*, IV, 11.

42. Ibid., norm. 3.

43. Ibid., IV, 8.

44. Cf. James 5:15 and 1 John 5:16.

Unfortunately, all too many Catholics have neglected to make use of these spiritual resources. Indulgences not only help us grow in holiness but they also place us in solidarity with our Lord, the Blessed Mother, the saints in heaven, and the souls in Purgatory in the continuing work of sanctification. One of the challenges of Vatican II was "the universal call to holiness."[45] At the heart of holiness is charity, and the perfection of charity is the ultimate rationale and end of the Catholic doctrine of indulgences. We pray that Dr. Peters' guide will help the faithful make better use of indulgences as a wonderful means of growth toward spiritual perfection.

Robert Fastiggi, PHD
Sacred Heart Major Seminary, Detroit, MI

---

45. Cf. *Lumen gentium*, 39–42.

Chapter 1

A Brief Overview
of Indulgences

The changes that have swept through the Church in recent decades—changes affecting liturgy, education, religious life, and the lay apostolate, to name but a few—have been startling. One of the more regrettable, if unavoidable, effects of these changes has been to deprive today's Catholics of a set of common experiences that are shared across generational lines and that in turn could be reflected in a common vocabulary. Consequently, when it comes to discussing a topic such as "indulgences," it makes a great deal of difference what age group is being addressed.

With Catholics, say, 60 and older, one can safely assume they have some memory of indulgences and might have even retained, albeit in a vague way, the practice of "offering something up for the poor souls." While they are unlikely to know the theology behind indulgences, they understand indulgences to be something good and, at least once reminded of them, worth striving for. In contrast, most Catholics under 40 (except the very curious) will have never heard of indulgences and, if they have heard of indulgences, would vaguely assume them to be one of those embarrassing medievalisms that the Church quietly shelved after Vatican II. Finally, the middle group, those from about 40 to 60, is in perhaps the worst position, for they are close enough to the lived experience of indulgences to sense that they have missed out on something, but are too young to have a Catholic awareness of where to go to find out the real story.

There is no sense in crying over spilt milk, and we have to start somewhere. So we begin with an overview of indulgences, frankly admitting that what might be boringly obvious to some might be amazingly revelatory to others. If the overview of indulgences provided in this chapter is enough, one should feel free to skip to Chapter Five of this book where the indulgences now in force are discussed. If, however, one wants to delve more deeply into the theology and discipline of indulgences, one might do well to move prayerfully through Chapters Two through Four at one's own pace.

What Is an Indulgence?

We begin with a very simple question: *What is an indulgence?* We find a very simple answer: *An indulgence is a way to reduce the amount of punishment one has to undergo for sins.*

Even this simple, straightforward answer contains, however, several assumptions that might be missed or, if noticed, might be challenged. To start with, it assumes that we commit sins and that God notices them. It assumes that sin, besides being something wrong in itself and to be avoided for that reason, also results in some sort of actual punishment, and that we as individuals will personally owe something to that punishment. Finally, it assumes that something we can do here and now could mitigate that punishment, and maybe even eliminate it. Each of these important points is discussed in this book, but for right now, let us stay focused on indulgences themselves.

Indulgences are applied only to sins that have been forgiven, so there should be no misunderstanding that indulgences "let people off" from sin without admitting they have done something wrong and seeking forgiveness for it, and even less, that indulgences are a way of getting advanced permission to sin. It does raise, though, a question as to *how* a sin can be forgiven, yet some punishment still be owed for it.

An indulgence is granted only through the Catholic Church, though that does not necessarily imply that only Catholics can obtain indulgences, or at least certain indulgences, and what special considerations might be apply in their case. *Most indulgences are available to any baptized person who, with proper dispositions (chiefly, sorrow for sin), carefully performs the works described by an indulgence.*

One can apply the good of an indulgence either for one's own benefit or for that of the faithful departed, but not for another living member of the Church. But what exactly that benefit is and how one can be sure of having obtained it (or of having given it to a soul suffering in purgatory) remains to be seen.

The simple fact is that one need not understand *how* indulgences work in order to make them an effective part of a healthy spiritual life any more than one needs to understand *how* the bio-chemistry of nutrition works in order to benefit from healthy foods. Put another way, it's usually best to do what your mother (including Mother Church) tells you, even when you're not sure why. Briefly, all that a Christian needs do to obtain an indulgence is to express to Our Lord, in these or similar words, "Lord, in sorrow for my sins which you have for-given, I wish to obtain the indulgences You now offer me, and I offer this work or prayer in that spirit." That is really all there is to it.

For the information presented in the pages that follow, we will draw on basically four official sources that contain the Church's teaching and discipline on indulgences. Those sources are:

Canon Law

Current ecclesiastical law on indulgences is found in Canons 992–997 of the 1983 Code of Canon Law.[1]

Special Pontifical Law

In his apostolic constitution *Indulgentiarum doctrina* (hereafter, *Doctrina*),[2] Pope Paul VI thoroughly reorganized the modern eccle-siastical discipline on indulgences. *Doctrina* is very important for understanding current Church law on indulgences and for its treat-ment of several related matters not covered by the 1983 Code. The translations of *Doctrina* used here are mine.[3] Pope John Paul II has

---

1. *Codex Iuris Canonici auctoritate Ioannis Pauli PP. II promulgatus* (Rome: Typis Polyglottis Vaticanis, 1983), hereafter 1983 CIC. The translations of the 1983 Code used here are mine. An English translation of the 1983 Code is available in *Code of Canon Law: Latin-English Edition, New English Translation* (Washington, D.C.: Canon Law Society of America, 1999). The prior ecclesiastical law on indulgences was found chiefly in Canons 911–936 of the 1917 Code of Canon Law (hereafter, 1917 CIC), an English translation of which is available in E. Peters, *The 1917 or Pio-Benedictine Code of Canon Law in English translation with extensive scholarly apparatus* (San Francisco: Ignatius Press, 2000).

2. Paul VI, apostolic constitution, *Indulgentiarum doctrina*, 1 January 1967, *Acta Apostolicae Sedis* 59 (1967), pp. 5–24.

3. Other English translations of *Doctrina* can be found in International Commission on English in the Liturgy, *Documents on the Liturgy 1963–1979* (Collegeville, MN: Liturgical Press, 1982), pp. 995–1009, and, slightly adapted, in *The Handbook of Indulgences* (Catholic Book Publishing, 1991) pp. 99–121. A summary and partial translation of *Doctrina* can also

made some minor additions to the pontifical law regulating indulgences. These will be pointed out as they are encountered.

Curial Regulations

The Apostolic Penitentiary, an office of the Roman Curia, regulates the administration of indulgences chiefly through the publication of its *Enchiridion indulgentiarum: normae et concessiones*, or "Handbook on Indulgences." Consequent to Paul VI's reorganization of indulgences, four editions of the Enchiridion have been published: first on June 29, 1968; then as slightly revised in October 1968; as more significantly revised on May 18, 1986; and finally as revised and significantly reorganized in 1999.[4] The *Enchiridion Indulgentiarum 1999/2004* (Roma: Libreria Editrice Vaticana, 2004), although not yet available in English, contains some minor additions over the 1999 version, and is the version studied herein.[5]

Catechetical Presentation

The current official catechetical presentation of indulgences is found in the *Catechism of the Catholic Church*, 2d ed., (hereafter, CCC) nos.

be found in *Canon Law Digest 6*: 570–575. Yet another English translation is available on the Vatican website, www.vatican.va.

4. A translation of the original (but now superseded) June 1968 norms (but not the prayers or works themselves) can be found in *Canon Law Digest 7*: 675–681. A translation of the revised (but now superseded) October 1968 version of the norms, prayers, and works appeared as W. Barry, trans., *Enchiridion of Indulgences, Norms and Grants*, (New York: Catholic Book Publishing, 1969). An English translation of the entire 1986 Enchiridion (now superseded) is available in *The Handbook of Indulgences* (New York: Catholic Book Publishing, 1991).

5. Prior to the post-conciliar reorganization of indulgences, the Apostolic Penitentiary published various editions of its Enchiridion (variously titled), or approved others doing so. The most common English title of these works was *The Raccolta* (sometimes misidentified by others as the "Racolata"). The final pre-conciliar edition of the Enchiridion, based on the 1950 Latin *editio typica*, appeared in English as J. Christopher, et al., eds., *The Raccolta or a Manual of Indulgences* (Benziger Brothers, 1957) herein, Raccolta. While these older versions of the Enchiridion or Raccolta are no longer in force per *Doctrina*, norm 20, and hence they no longer confer the benefits of indulgences on those who might still use them, they do provide some useful perspectives for understanding the modern discipline on indulgences.

The Second Vatican Council made no statements on the subject of indulgences. Shortly before the Council closed, however, the conciliar Fathers were presented with an extensive study of indulgences, supervised by Fernando Cardinal Cento, that Pope Paul VI had commissioned on 24 July 1963, and were invited to send their comments on it to Rome. Many did so. Cf. Palmer & Tavard, 439. These materials are available in *Acta Synodalia Sacrosanctae Concilii Oecumenici Vaticani II (Typis Polyglottis Vaticanis, 1978)*, vol. IV, Part VI, pp. 131–197, 291–307, and 315–336.

1471–1479. The translations of the Catechism used here are mine. Indulgences were not treated in the Catechism of the Council of Trent.

REQUIREMENTS FOR OBTAINING INDULGENCES

To obtain a *partial* indulgence, as often as one wants, one must:

1. Be baptized
2. Be in the state of grace
3. Have the intention to obtain the indulgence
4. Perform the works or offer prayers correctly

To obtain a plenary indulgence, usually at most once per day, one must:

1. Meet all the requirements for a partial indulgence
2. Not be excommunicated
3. Have no affection for sin, not even venial sin
4. Receive the Sacrament of Reconciliation and Holy Communion and offer prayers of the pope's intention within the prescribed period of time

At this point, then, one can either go to Chapter Five of this volume for a presentation of indulgenced prayers and works,[6] or one can continue reading for a more detailed explanation of the great gift of indulgences in preparation for making them a part of one's spiritual life or improving upon the practices one has already acquired.[7]

Then again, as will be explained in the following pages, the more one brings to the practice of indulgences, especially by way of

---

6. The indulgences attached to these prayers and works are known as grants or, more technically, "concessions," abbreviated herein as "conc."

7. One thing, however, a faithful Catholic is not permitted to do: to doubt or deny the authority of the Church in the matter of indulgences. While there is no ecclesiastical command to make use of the gift of indulgences (*Doctrina*, no. 11), they are a firm part of Church doctrine, and may not be rejected by the faithful, however neglected these gifts might be. See CCC 1471–1479 and the Council of Trent, Session 25, Chapter XXI, Decree concerning Indulgences: "Since the power of granting indulgences was conferred by Christ on the Church (Matthew 16:19, John 20:23) and she has even in the earliest times made use of that power divinely given to her, the holy council teaches and commands that the use of indulgences, most salutary to the Christian people and approved by the authority of the holy councils, is to be retained in the Church, and it condemns with anathema those who assert that they are useless or deny that there is in the Church the power of granting them." H. Schroeder, trans., *The Canons and Decrees of the Council of Trent* (Tan, 1978), pp. 253–254. See also *Doctrina*, no. 1.

increased understanding, the more can derive from them. Even if, therefore, one already has a solid grasp of the foregoing essentials, it might still be beneficial to take some time to review some of the deeper explanations that follow, if only to augment one's appreciation for the great gift from God that indulgences are.

Chapter 2

The Context of Indulgences: Repairing the Damage of Sins

An Overview of Sin

The Catholic Church's basic teaching on indulgences is quite brief.[1] While scholarly research on indulgences would eventually lead one into such fields as "Christology" (the systematic study of Christ and his works) and "soteriology" (the specific study of the mystery of salvation), historically speaking, indulgences grew up alongside pastoral practices related to the sacrament of Confession, which helped keep the explanations of indulgences readily understandable to the faithful.[2] Only in more recent centuries did the Church, faced with numerous controversies and misunderstandings in connection with indulgences, need to elaborate what might seem to be a more complicated definition of an indulgence. But for all that, an indulgence is still a simple thing that can be readily understood and applied in one's life of faith. Basically, indulgences are a generous way that God offers us to repair the damage

---

1. The Catechism of the Catholic Church needs just nine paragraphs (CCC 1471–1479) to set forth most of the Church's teaching on indulgences. That's barely two pages in a work that runs nearly 1,000 pages total. The 1983 Code of Canon Law regulates the practice of indulgences in just six canons (1983 CIC 992–997) out of a total of 1,752 canons. One could easily read both of these passages in fifteen minutes.

2. *Doctrina*, nos. 6–7. Even today, both the Catechism of the Catholic Church and the 1983 Code discuss indulgences immediately after setting forth Church discipline on sacramental Confession. Of course, the *scholarly* literature on indulgences is vast, it having had several centuries to develop, including many in which indulgences were highly controverted. To cite any of those works risks wrongly signaling a preference for one or two sources over many other fine ones. Nevertheless, two treatises provide reliable overviews of much that preceded them, namely, Seraphinus de Angelis, *De Indulgentiis: Tractatus quoad earum naturam and usum* [Treatise on the nature and use of indulgences], 2d ed. (Libreria Editrice Vaticana, 1950), herein, de Angelis, all translations mine; and Francis Hagedorn, *General Legislation on Indulgences*, Canon Law Studies no. 22 (J.C.D. thesis, Catholic University of America, 1924), herein, Hagedorn.

of personal sin in our lives. [3] But to appreciate this explanation, we will need to have a clearer understanding of what sin itself is.

When we sin—and we all sin (CCC 1847)—we do what should be unthinkable, namely, we offend the majesty and sanctity of God.[4] Moreover, we damage, and sometimes destroy, the friendship that God desires between us and him, we make ourselves more susceptible to sin in the future, and we attack the bonds of communion that we as baptized persons are meant to share with each other as members of Christ's Mystical Body or Church (CCC 1846–1851). Even our small sins (to say nothing of our grave sins) are so terribly contrary to God's holiness that, if we had been left to ourselves, we could never, even in a lifetime of penance, make up for so much as one of them. Only a God—if I may put it that way—could pay the awful price of our sins that was needed to repair the affront that sin represents to divine majesty and holiness, and to restore us to divine friendship. That reparation is exactly what Our Lord did for us when he suffered death on the Cross.[5] In fact, not only did Christ pay our sin debt for us, but the merits that he won on Calvary infinitely *exceeded* the debt of sin we have all accumulated. And this inexhaustible "treasury of merit"—for that is what it truly is, a treasury of the accomplishments of Christ[6]—has been entrusted by the Lord to his Church for our benefit (CCC 1476; 1983 CIC 992).

But while it is true to say that, on our own, we had no hope of repairing the damage caused by our sins and that we are completely dependent on the merits of Jesus Christ to save us, that does *not* imply that God does not want our cooperation in his plan for our salvation or, in other words, that he will pay our sin debt for us without some effort or cooperation on our part. As Saint Augustine observed over 1,500 years ago, God created us without our consent but he will not save us without our consent (CCC 1847). For Christians, this "cooperation"

---

3. Personal sins are those we commit by our own choices, thoughts, words, actions, or omissions. Original Sin, on the other hand, while it is real and has real effects, is not incurred by our own choice and is not addressed by indulgences. Original Sin is cleansed in the sacrament of Baptism and not in the sacrament of Confession, in which context indulgences first appeared and to which they are still closely connected. We will discuss these points in more detail later.

4. *Doctrina*, no. 2.

5. *Doctrina*, no. 5.

6. *Doctrina*, no. 5.

(from the Latin meaning "to *work* together") in their own salvation formally begins when we receive Baptism and become heirs to the infinite merits of Jesus Christ (CCC 1265; 1983 CIC 96, 204–205). After Baptism, a Christian's continuing cooperation in God's salvific plan is manifested by, among other things, living a life of charity, making regular use of the sacrament of Confession, and practicing penance, all according to the teachings of Christ and his Church. And it is here that the generosity God shows to us in the form of indulgences can be better understood.

So desirous is God for our complete reconciliation with him, and so eager is he to encourage in us even the smallest acts of love and penance of which he makes us capable, that he willingly accepts in reparation for our sins not only the merits that these small efforts already have in his eyes, but, according to the discipline laid down by his Church, he is also willing to accept on our behalf those *additional* shares in the merits won by Christ and now entrusted to the Church, shares that we call "indulgences."[7] Indulgences are thus one of the ways that God gives us to speed our return with him, and they are a valuable means to deepen our life of love for God and one another.

Precisely because indulgences are one way that God gives us for addressing some of the effects of personal sin in our lives, we must now consider certain aspects of personal sin in order to understand better what indulgences can, and cannot, accomplish.

TYPES OF PERSONAL SIN

There are many ways to analyze or explain the concept of personal sin (CCC 1853), but broadly speaking, personal sin falls into two main categories, mortal and venial (CCC 1854–1864). Both kinds of personal sin are contrary to God's plan for us and both should be avoided, but they nevertheless differ in some important ways.

---

7. Strictly speaking, the "merit" that one deserves for having performed a good action cannot be transferred to another, but to the degree that such good actions also result in some satisfaction toward one's punishment for sins, those satisfactions can be applied on behalf of another. As Hagedorn, at p. 53, puts it: "There can be no vicarious merit. On the other hand, there is vicarious satisfaction, that is, the offering of one person's satisfactions in payment for another's debt of punishment." An indulgence augments not the "merit" of an action, but rather its worth in regard to the satisfaction of punishment owed as a result of sin, and thus indulgences can be applied to another's (specifically, the dead's) benefit under certain conditions.

Mortal sin (sometimes called "grave" or "serious" sin) is the deliberate and free choice to engage in a significant moral evil (CCC 1851–1861). Mortal sin kills the life of charity in one's soul.[8] Mortal sin destroys one's friendship with God and severs the bonds of communion that each baptized person has with all the others.[9] To die in mortal sin means to exist thereafter in a state forever separated from God, an indescribable torment known as hell (CCC 1033–1037, 1861, 1874). The eternal punishment that would occur for dying with even a single unforgiven mortal sin is beyond describing.

Venial sin (sometimes called "light" or "daily" sin[10]), on the other hand, damages but does not destroy the life of grace in one's soul (CCC 1863). It puts, as it were, a distance between us and God, who wants nothing else than to have us as close as possible (closer to him than we can ever imagine). Venial sin leaves us weaker in the face of future temptations and loosens, but does not break, the bonds of communion that we share with all the baptized. Venial sin hampers, but does not stop, our ability to move toward God. To die with unforgiven venial sin on one's soul means that one's punishment in the next life will be severe,[11] but we know that such punishment will eventually come to an end, and everlasting union with God will be obtained (CCC 1030–1032). We can briefly summarize the two types of personal sins in Table 2.1.

---

8. Mortal sin does not, as it is sometimes mistakenly claimed, "kill the soul" because the soul is immortal and *cannot* die (CCC 366). The life of grace in one's soul, on the other hand, a supernatural sharing in the life of the Blessed Trinity, *can* be destroyed by certain sins (CCC 1997–1998).

9. Mortal sin does not cancel one's baptism because the seal or character of baptism is indelible and cannot be erased (CCC 1272-1274, 1983 CIC 845). Nor does mortal sin exempt one from the authority of the Church (indeed, not even excommunication does that) but it does deprive one of the benefit of being joined in full communion with the Mystical Body of Christ (CCC 1861). See also *Doctrina*, no. 4.

10. *Doctrina*, no. 3.

11. Saint Thomas Aquinas, drawing on Saint Augustine, says that the least pain in purgatory is worse than the worst pain here on earth. ST, App. 1, Q.2, art. 1. See also, R. Bastien, "Purgatory", *New Catholic Encyclopedia* (McGraw-Hill, 1967), vol. 11, pp. 1034–1039 [hereafter, Bastien]. Saint Thomas, of course, had no interest in frightening people or in painting a gruesome picture of a vengeful God, but he did want us to have a sense of how offensive sin is in God's eyes, how much his holiness is affronted by our evil, and therefore what an incalculable gift Christ gave us when he offered his own life as ransom for our sins.

Table 2.1   Types of Personal Sin

Mortal Sin	Venial Sin
Destroys the life of grace in the soul	Weakens the life of grace in the soul
Cannot be forgiven after death	Can be forgiven after death
Deserves terrible eternal punishment	Deserves hard but limited punishment

EFFECTS OF PERSONAL SIN: GUILT AND PUNISHMENT

Every personal sin, regardless of whether it is mortal or venial, has two immediate effects. It is very important to keep in mind the distinction between these two effects of sin because the remedies for these different effects are themselves very different. In brief, the first effect of sin, what is called the "liability of guilt," can be remedied only by *forgiveness*, while the second effect of sin, the "liability of punishment," can only be remedied by *satisfaction*.[12]

Simply put, the first effect of sin is that we become *guilty* in God's eyes, that is, we become the personally responsible agents or doers of moral evil.[13] This is called the "liability of guilt" or "guiltiness."[14] This first effect of sin, liability of guilt before God, can be remedied only by forgiveness from God (CCC 1441). We cannot forgive ourselves

---

12. In older literature, one might encounter the term "satispassion" to denote hardships borne in this life or paid in Purgatory as punishment for sin, and "satisfaction" to describe works legitimately offered in place of such sufferings. See e.g., Hagedorn, p. 50. The distinction, while useful, has been lost in common parlance and is not observed in this presentation.

13. This is, by the way, yet another way to distinguish Original Sin, for which we bear no responsibility (although we do bear its consequences), from our personal sins, for which we are responsible. Indulgences, as we shall see, operate only in regard to personal sins. Moreover, only God knows how much any specific individual is *actually* responsible for his or her personal sins. It is certainly possible that some persons at some times, while they have certainly committed objectively grave offenses, are not personally responsible for those sins, or are only partially responsible for them, in God's eyes. Hence the frequent admonitions against judging one another lest we pretend to a depth of knowledge about particular cases that only God can have. Whatever the degree of one's personal responsibility for sin might be, however, to the same degree one is *guilty* of personal sin and liable to punishment for it. See CCC 1859–1860.

14. One of the most common signs of "guiltiness" is, of course, *shame*, a feeling of unworthiness before God. While the feeling of shame is not pleasant, it is a sign that our conscience is at work in us, calling us to seek reconciliation with God. It is very important continually to inform one's conscience correctly in accord with the mind of the Church, and then not to ignore it. Certainly, there are people who suffer from "scrupulosity" and mistakenly believe that they are at odds with God when actually they are not, but there are far more people who ignore their conscience or misshape it to avoid "feeling guilty" for sin.

of sin, and we cannot obtain this forgiveness from anyone else beside God.[15] An indulgence has nothing to do with addressing this first effect of sin, that is, with obtaining *forgiveness* for this "liability of guilt." We'll discuss this in more detail shortly, but just now we need to look at the second effect of sin because that is the effect upon which indulgences work.

The second effect of sin, again regardless of whether those sins were venial or mortal, is that we become subject to *punishment* for our sins. This "liability of punishment" can take a variety of forms, including even the suffering that a Christian feels when he or she recognizes deep inside an increased proclivity to sin as a result of earlier sins (CCC 1472). Fundamentally, though, because sin has as its chief wrong the rejection of God who is all good and deserving of all our love, some restitution is owed toward the divine goodness and order that we have marred by sin. This personal share in punishment, though just a tiny fraction of the punishment that we really deserve for offending the unimaginable sanctity of God, must be addressed—either during this life or in the next—if we are ultimately to enter into the presence of God. It is toward this second consequence of sin, the liability of punishment, that indulgences can, under certain conditions, make satisfaction. We can summarize our discussion so far in Table 2.2.

Table 2.2   Effects of Sin

Liability of Guilt	Liability of Punishment
Only remedy is forgiveness	Made once and for all by Christ
Can be granted only by God, and comes directly or through his ministers	though individuals should cooperate with him

Several important points flow from what we have discussed so far. One of the most important implications of the difference between the liability of guilt and the liability of punishment is this: *Punishment* for sins can never be satisfied while *guilt* for those sins remains

---

15. Strictly speaking, the Church does not forgive us our sins against God, but rather, she is the divinely authorized means that God normally uses to forgive us our offenses against him (1983 CIC 959). Recall, though, that all sins attack, and some sins destroy, our communion with the Church, and in this sense our reconciliation with the Church must also be made. Of course, if our sin has directly offended another person—and obviously many sins do—we can and should seek forgiveness from that other person also, though that does not lessen our need for forgiveness from God.

unforgiven. As long as one has unforgiven sin on one's soul, that is, as long as one is *guilty* before God of some sins, the merits of Christ will not be applied against the liability of *punishment* for those sins. One cannot atone, even in token amount, for unforgiven sins.[16] That is why indulgences, a special application of the merits of Jesus Christ toward our liability of punishment for sin, cannot be obtained for sins whose guilt is not yet forgiven. *No* atonement for *unforgiven* sins is ever possible. Period.

Another important consequence of the distinction between the liability of guilt and the liability of punishment is this: *Guilt* for sin can be forgiven while some consequences or *punishment* for that sin yet remains (CCC 1459). An analogy might be useful here.

In deliberately smashing my brother's expensive radio, I have violated his rights of ownership, shown contempt for his person and feelings, and deprived him of a costly radio. Later, if (as I should) I seek his forgiveness for my action, he can (and ought) to extend his forgiveness to me for the affronts that I inflicted on him. But he is still entitled to expect me to replace, at least to the extent I can, the radio I destroyed. We call this particular obligation the duty of "restitution" and to the extent that restitution *can* be made for an offense (say, by returning stolen property or by retracting a slander[17]) one is obligated to try to do so. Similarly, even our smallest sins are offenses against God, his majesty, his sanctity, indeed, the very order

---

16. There are two grounds for confusion here, one substantive, one terminological, so let us address them both right away. First, substantively, one might well have unforgiven venial sins on one's soul when striving to obtain an indulgence. Because venial sin does not cast one out of the state of grace, it is still possible to obtain an indulgence toward the liability of punishment for one's *earlier forgiven* mortal or venial sins, albeit not for the unforgiven venial sins one still carries. We'll discuss shortly a good way of addressing this matter, but we should immediately note that, if one is in the state of mortal sin, one *cannot* obtain any indulgence whatsoever, even an indulgence toward one's earlier *forgiven* sins.

Second, on a more terminological level, what we here call "satisfaction" was called by some earlier writers "reconciliation" and referred only to how *punishment* for sins, not forgiveness for sins, was addressed. See generally Hagedorn, pp. 13–21. But because today the sacrament of Confession is often called "Reconciliation" and describes, of course, the process by which *guilt* for sin, not punishment for sin, is addressed, confusion might arise when reading older treatises on indulgences if one encounters the term "reconciliation" being used in the sense of addressing punishment for sin rather than forgiveness for sins. Just remember, it is an older usage which would not be recommended today.

17. For a specific canonical example of this requirement, see 1983 CIC 982, where, in the case of the very serious offense of falsely accusing a confessor of solicitation, absolution for that sin cannot be granted until there is formal retraction of the charge. See also 1983 CIC 1390 § 3.

he put into the universe. We can be forgiven the guilt that we incurred in sinning, yet, to the degree that God makes us able, we should strive to make some (albeit small) restitution for our sins, including the acceptance of whatever punishment he justly imposes. Of course, God already helps us with his grace to bear the punishments he imposes, but through indulgences as applied by his Church, he helps us all the more!

In yet another way, the differences that we outlined between mortal sin and venial sin are especially important because, when it comes to the liability of punishment, mortal sins and venial sin differ very significantly.

The guilt attached to mortal sin is *so* profound that the punishment due for it in divine justice should be—and actually is—eternal (CCC 1861). Thus, if God were applying to us *only* his perfect justice to us, many would never see him face to face. Because of this, when God extends his merciful forgiveness to us who confess mortal sins, his forgiveness not only removes the liability of guilt we bear for mortal sin, but he also forgives (more specifically, he accepts the infinite merits of Christ toward) the liability for *eternal* punishment that our mortal sins deserves.[18] But, in place of the liability for *eternal* punishment that, in strict justice, should have been ours, God leaves us with a liability for some *temporal* punishment that, just like the punishment due for venial sins, must somehow be satisfied.[19]

Another very important aspect of the difference between the liability of guilt and the liability of punishment is this: While

---

18. "[S]ince the state of sanctifying grace thus restored in Confession [or by a perfect act of contrition] is incompatible with liability to eternal punishment, the pardon of guilt imparted by Confession [or by a perfect act of contrition] necessarily brings with it the cancellation of the eternal penalty due to sin." Hagedorn, p. 46.

19. One can safely assume that the liability for temporal punishment that God imposes on us for forgiven mortal sins (whose liability for punishment should have been ours eternally) is heavier than the liability of punishment we owe for our forgiven venial sins. In this context, though, the phrase "temporal punishment" can cause some confusion. When discussing indulgences, the term "temporal" should be understood as contrasting with "eternal." Thus, mortal sin is said to deserve "eternal" punishment, whereas venial sin only warrants "temporal" (or better, "temporary") punishment. "Temporal" does *not* mean only "this worldly." Therefore, "temporal" punishment for sin can be carried out in this life *or* the next. "Eternal" punishment, of necessity, can only be carried out in the next life, or else it would not eternal. This aspect of "eternal" punishments being applied in the next life makes some people mistakenly assume that "temporal" punishments must be carried out in this life. They do not; some "temporal" punishments can be imposed in the next life (i.e., in Purgatory, as noted in CCC 1031, 1472).

forgiveness of guilt can only be granted by God and satisfaction for the punishment due for our sins can only be made by Christ, God, nevertheless, accepts not only our own small actions in reparation for sin, but also under certain conditions, he also accepts the actions of others on our behalf. Saint Paul was perhaps the first one to put words to this concept when he said: "What is lacking in the sufferings of Christ I make up for in my own body" (Colossians 1:24).[20] Now, obviously, nothing was lacking in the sufferings of Christ, except this: Paul was not suffering *with* him. Christ wants our cooperation in working out our own salvation, and in contributing to others (i.e. the dead) who are working out theirs. And just as we can draw on other members of the Body of Christ for help in bearing the punishments due to our sins, so too, under certain circumstances, can we lend to other members of the Church our help in carrying their burdens.

Forgiveness for Personal Sins

Indulgences do not obtain forgiveness for sins, and they do not apply toward punishment that is due for unforgiven sins. So, we need to be clear on how God extends his merciful forgiveness to us in the first place, before we can talk in more detail about how he makes possible the mitigation of the punishment that is due for those sins.

Broadly speaking, there are two ways to obtain from God forgiveness for the guilt of our personal sins:[21] (1) forgiveness can be obtained through the use of the sacraments Christ gave his Church, or, (2) in certain cases, it can be obtained outside of the Sacraments. The manner of forgiveness varies somewhat with the type of sin for which forgiveness is sought, so we will look at venial and mortal sins separately.

---

20. Consider also Saint Paul's words "Bear one another's burdens and so fulfill the law of Christ." Galatians 6:2.

21. Notice, again, that we do not speak about Original Sin here, for that is dealt with in Baptism, and is not addressed in the matter of indulgences.

Ways of Obtaining Forgiveness for Venial Sins

Personal contrition. The ordinary manner of seeking and receiving God's forgiveness for *venial* sins is to express, directly to God, in spoken words or even just conscious thoughts, one's sorrow for such sins and one's resolution to avoid them, with God's help, in the future (CCC 1451–1454). Moreover, any act of charity undertaken in sorrow for sin also suffices for obtaining God's forgiveness for venial sins (CCC 1863, 1875). Because venial sins are for most of us very common, one should develop the habit of frequently, but at least once a day, expressing sorrow to God for having committed venial sins, and of asking him for the grace to avoid them in the future.

Sacramental Confession. An especially praiseworthy manner of seeking forgiveness for venial sins and petitioning the grace to avoid them in the future, a way long recommended by the Church, is to bring them to sacramental confession (CCC 1458; 1983 CIC 988 § 2). Besides obtaining for us sacramental graces, bringing sins, even venial sins, to Confession makes it possible for us to receive specific advice on dealing with sin in our lives and offers us an occasion to exercise a healthy humility.[22] In any case, forgiveness for venial sins sought in any of these ways is obtained immediately and whatever the liability for punishment that God leaves for those forgiven sins can then be atoned for by the individual or remitted in whole or in part by an indulgence.

---

22. Strictly speaking, the reception of any sacrament or sacramental (CCC 1667–1679) while venial sins remain on the soul is an acceptable way to obtain forgiveness for such sins and to move closer to God. Of course, one must be very careful not to misconstrue this point in such a way as to permit the reception of sacraments in the state of mortal sin. One should not approach any other sacrament, especially the Eucharist, while in the state of mortal sin (see 1983 CIC 916, including its narrow exceptions). While reception of the Eucharist by one in venial sin can be the occasion of obtaining forgiveness of those small sins, receiving the Eucharist (or Confirmation, Matrimony, or Holy Orders) while in the state of mortal sin is sacrilegious and, objectively speaking, adds another mortal sin to the soul.

A special case of post-baptismal forgiveness for venial sins within a sacrament is Anointing of the Sick. Venial sins are forgiven by the reception of the Sacrament of Anointing, certainly if the recipient of the sacrament makes that desire known (even to God alone) at the time, but also even if the recipient is unable to ask for the sacrament or to express sorrow for sin at the time of anointing, provided that he or she has been in the habit of leading the Christian life, from which it can be reasonably inferred that the sacrament and all its benefits would have been desired (1983 CIC 1006). The sacrament of Anointing cannot be celebrated for those who persist in manifest grave sin (1983 CIC 1007). It is pastorally preferable, but not required, to celebrate also the sacrament of Confession with the one seeking Anointing of the Sick, and if possible also to join Anointing with reception of the Eucharist (CCC 1517).

Obtaining Forgiveness for Mortal Sins

Because the deadly character of serious or grave sin differs from the character of venial sins, the manner of obtaining forgiveness for mortal sin also differs in some important respects from the methods suitable for lighter sin.

Confession. The only ordinary, post-baptismal manner for seeking and receiving forgiveness for mortal sins is in individual sacramental Confession (CCC 1456–1457; 1983 CIC 960). There is no other ordinary manner of obtaining forgiveness of mortal sins other than through the sacrament of Confession. When we speak of confession here, we mean the one-on-one (whether anonymous or face-to-face does not matter) method of receiving the *sacrament* of Confession, or General Absolution, even if it is done illicitly (CCC 1483; 1983 CIC 960–963). We do not mean "penance services" *per se* or the Confiteor (the "I confess to almighty God" prayers said during Mass), for, though praiseworthy in themselves and indisputably effective against venial sin, neither of those activities qualify as sacramental Confession.

Perfect Act of Contrition. The extraordinary manner of post-baptismal forgiveness for mortal sins is received by what is known as a "perfect act of contrition." The notion of "perfect," in this context, does not mean "flawless" or "pristine" but rather "complete" or "with no necessary elements missing." Also, precisely because it is *contrition* we are talking about, the sorrow for sin must be based on the individual's recognition that sin is fundamentally an affront to the sanctity of God. It is not sufficient that one's sorrow be motivated by *attrition*, that is, a fear of punishment (for example, the loss of heaven or the pains of hell). Moreover, those who receive forgiveness through such a "perfect act of contrition" are still bound to approach the Sacrament of Confession as soon as possible thereafter (CCC 1483; 1983 CIC 963). We may summarize the ways of obtaining forgiveness for personal sin in Table 2.3.

As we discussed at the outset of this book, it is not necessary to understand in detail exactly how God forgives our sins or what methods he has given us to be reconciled with him in order to benefit from the gift of indulgences. However, having a better understanding of these concepts cannot but help to deepen our gratitude to God

Table 2.3   Forgiveness of the Liability of Guilt for Sin which comes only
from God

Can be obtained sacramentally through		Can be obtained extra-sacramentally through	
Sacrament of Baptism[23]	Sacrament of Reconciliation	Sufficient sorrow *or* penitent charity	Perfect contrition[24] *and* the intention promptly to confess sacramentally
forgives Original Sin Personal Sins	forgives Personal Sins	forgives only Venial Sins	forgives Mortal Sins (and other Venial Sins)

for having taken on the burden of sins precisely so that we could be
reunited with him. At this point, we are ready to turn our attention
to how indulgences specifically contribute to our reconciliation
with God and the best way to do that will be to analyze just what
an indulgence is.

---

23. Baptism is a special case of forgiveness for sins and, as we have noted, it does not figure in
the discussion of indulgences. Nevertheless, for the sake of clarity: For infants, baptism removes
the stain of Original Sin and makes them co-heirs in the redemption won by Jesus Christ; for
anyone over the age of reason, baptism not only removes Original Sin, but also the guilt for any
mortal and venial sins they might have committed up to that time, as well as from all liability
of punishment they owed for any personal sins committed up to that point. (CCC 1263.)

24. Hagedorn expressly holds "perfect contrition" sufficient in regard to indulgences:
"There is in the law no specification of the means to be employed in putting oneself in the
state of grace. Confession, the usual means, is not demanded. Therefore an act of perfect contrition is sufficient." Hagedorn, p. 87. We should not confuse this insight, however, with the
requirement of going to Confession that one finds associated with, say, plenary indulgences (see
Enchiridion 1999, no. 20 § 1). In those cases, sacramental Confession is an express requirement
that must be satisfied.

Chapter 3

A Formal Definition of an Indulgence

With the information on sin and forgiveness of guilt in mind, we can now consider how the second effect of sin, namely the "liability of punishment," is addressed by indulgences. An excellent way to do this is to examine directly the formal definition of an indulgence and to explain its various parts.[1] Canon 992 of the 1983 Code of Canon Law defines an indulgence thus:

> An indulgence is a remission before God of the temporal punishment for sins whose guilt is already forgiven, that a member of the Christian faithful, who is suitably disposed, under certain and definite conditions, obtains by the action of the Church that, as minister of redemption, dispenses and authoritatively applies the treasury of the satisfactions of Christ and of the saints.[2]

Already, several parts of this definition are clearer to us than when we started, but let us break it down into its parts and illuminate some of the rich teachings that underlie this careful definition. We will do this by examining sequentially the key words and phrases found in the definition.

---

1. The canonical definition of indulgence studied here is drawn from the definition used by Pope Paul VI in *Doctrina*, Norm 1. See also Enchiridion 1999, Norm 1; Enchiridion 1986, Norm 1. The Catechism's definition (see CCC 1471) is simply that of Pope Paul VI. The commentary offered here therefore applies to any of these versions of the definition.

2. 1983 CIC 992. Indulgentia est remissio coram Deo poenae temporalis pro peccatis, ad culpam quod attinet iam deletis, quam christifidelis, apte dispositus et certis ac definitis condicionibus, consequitur ope Ecclesiae quae, ut ministra redemptionis, thesaurum satisfactionum Christi et Sanctorum auctoritative dispensat et applicat. This terminology is substantively very close to that found in 1917 CIC 911, and thus one can fruitfully draw on canonical discussions of indulgences pre-dating the 1983 Code (such as Hagedorn and de Angelis) for insights into the current law (1983 CIC 6, 21).

An indulgence is a remission. We owe God an immense (and left on our own, unpayable) debt for sinfully offending his justice and holiness. But while God is willing to forgive the guilt of sin in us, he still expects us to shoulder with his grace some part of the debt of punishment (though in relation to what is actually owed, only a tiny part), either in this life by penance and works of charity or in the next life by bearing the trials of Purgatory. When we speak of indulgences as a "remission" of our punishments, we mean a reduction in the share of punishment for sin *we* would otherwise be bearing.[3] An important point needs to be made here: We should not think of indulgences as *canceling* some part of the debt owed to God, for in accord with God's infinite justice, offenses against God cannot simply be canceled; they must somehow be paid. Rather, an indulgence is the Church's application on our behalf of the merits of Jesus Christ precisely toward the debt of punishment we owe God.[4] As Saint Thomas explains it, one who gains an indulgence is not excused from the punishment of the debt of sin, but rather, is given the means of paying it.[5] Christ, who paid the full debt for our sins, shows his mercy yet again by helping us with indulgences granted through his Church to pay even the token amount of punishment for forgiven sins that in his love and justice he leaves with us.

A remission before God. While our personal sins certainly harm us and, directly or indirectly, harm others, sin is, first and foremost, an offense against the majesty and holiness of God, and it is to God that we owe our fundamental debt of sorrow and reparation (CCC 1850). Thus we say that the remission of the punishment owed as a penalty for forgiven sin obtained through indulgences is made "before God,"

---

3. Even the notion of "reduction" is difficult to express, for it suggests a reduction of "amount of punishment," or "severity of punishment," or even "time of punishment." Any of these notions might be completely accurate, or none of them might be, and the Church has not pronounced one way or the other. But whatever "reduction" or "remission" might suggest, an indulgence means that we undergo less punishment than we would have otherwise.

4. The analogy of a civil judge "commuting" a prison sentence might help, but keep in mind that when a judge commutes a convict's sentence, it is not as if someone else serves the time for the convict. If one considers God the Father as "commuting" all or part of our punishments for sin by way of an indulgence, it must be understood that God the Son still paid the full price for those sins.

5. *Summa Theologica*, Supp., Q. 25, a. 1. See also, *Doctrina*, no. 8, which reminds us that indulgences are not simply ways of paying one's sin debt, but also prompts one toward greater charity.

and not before some other authority.[6] Note that, if the forgiven sin to which an indulgence is being applied also occasioned an obligation on our part to make restitution, the fact that we might have obtained an indulgence toward the punishment that God imposes for that sin does *not* release us from the obligation that we might owe to others in this life.[7]

A remission before God of the temporal punishments. Indulgences are applied, as we have seen, only to what are called the temporal punishments for sin.[8] With the careful distinctions we made earlier, we recall that indulgences do not obtain *forgiveness* for sins, but only apply toward the temporal *punishments* for forgiven sins, whether that temporal punishment be for mortal sins (their eternal punishment already being remitted by God) or for venial sins, albeit in token amounts, and even then being bearable by us only with the grace of Christ. We will discuss later *how much* punishment for sins is remitted by an indulgence; for now, we only have to be clear, once again, that the indulgence remission applies only to punishment for sins, not to guilt.

Temporal punishments for sins whose guilt is forgiven. Reiterated here is a repudiation of one of the most persistent myths haunting the topic of indulgences, namely, the myth that an indulgence obtains *forgiveness* for sins. Forgiveness for sins is, as we have seen, obtained only from God either through sacramental Confession or, under certain circumstances, by a sufficient expression of sorrow for sin. An indulgence does not bring about the forgiveness of the guilt of sin, but rather, it operates in satisfaction (in whole or in part) of the debt of punishment that is still owed for sins that have already been forgiven. An indulgence cannot obtain remission of the liability of punishment for a sin that is not yet forgiven but only for those sins whose guilt is already forgiven.[9]

---

6. "Remission is said to be **before God** and not before the Church because an indulgence is not aimed at a penalty that is owed in light of [an earthly] judicial sentence; thus the penalty is satisfied not only in the external forum as administered by the Church, but also in the internal forum before God." De Angelis, no.2 (orig. emp.); See also 1983 CIC 992, 1917 CIC 911, and Hagedorn, pp. 51–52.

7. For example, if one steals money from an employer, confesses the sin, and receives absolution, and later obtains an indulgence with regard to the divine punishment owed for that sin, one is not thereby released from the obligation to make restitution for the theft.

8. De Angelis, no. 2.

9. Occasionally, in much older literature, one encounters the notion of indulgences as "absolving" from sin. To the degree that such terminology suggested that an indulgence freed

A member of the Christian faithful. Any baptized person is eligible to obtain (at least partial) indulgences.[10] Any Christian baptism suffices;[11] hence baptized non-Catholics are, in this regard at least, eligible to obtain indulgences.[12] Because baptism imprints an indelible character on the soul (CCC 1272; 1983 CIC 845 § 1), no one can, by any means, cancel or erase their baptism, although one might well squander the gift of grace it has conferred. Later, we will see that being in the state of grace is also necessary to obtain an indulgence, but for now we only

---

one from the *guilt* of sin, as opposed to the punishments arising from sin, that has *never* been accurate, as ecclesiastical writers have been careful to point out for many centuries. In each case, either the author using such ambiguous language simply did not know what he was talking about, or the terms in context clearly referred to "absolution" from the punishment of sin. In any event, such confusing phrases should not be used. See generally Hagedorn, pp. 47–49.

We might be seeing, albeit with less danger of serious misstatement, a modern example of such confusion in terminology when the sacrament of Confession or Reconciliation is sometimes referred to as the sacrament of Penance, thus facilitating confusion between the *sacrament* by which sins are forgiven, and the small *acts of expiation* imposed within the sacrament as a sign of one's willingness to make some amends for sins.

10. 1983 CIC 994 and 996 § 1; *Doctrina*, Norm 5; Enchiridion 1999, Norm 17 § 1; Enchiridion 1986 Norm 20 § 1, none of which uses the term "Catholic" in regard to eligibility for indulgences. Compare 1983 CIC 1170 by which non-Catholics may also receive blessings that were formerly restricted under 1917 CIC 1149. All authors agree that catechumens (as they are not baptized) may not benefit from indulgences (see, e.g., de Angelis, no. 52 and Hagedorn, p. 83), despite the advantages offered to them in other regards, such as their being eligible for blessings (1983 CIC 1170) and for Christian burial (1983 CIC 1183 § 1).

11. Generally, baptism with water made "In the name of the Father, and of the Son, and of the Holy Spirit" makes one a Christian (CCC 1239–1240; 1983 CIC 849). Recently, however, the Congregation for the Doctrine of the Faith declared Mormon baptism invalid, even though it recites the Trinitarian formula (5 June 2001, AAS 93 [2001] p. 476). Thus, Mormons (unless they have been baptized in another Christian denomination) are not Christians and are ineligible to receive indulgences. Also not eligible for indulgences, of course, are Jews, Moslems, and Hindus, all of whom lack baptism.

12. Non-Catholics are now eligible to receive, for example, under certain circumstances at least, several of the spiritual and religious benefits that earlier were reserved for Catholics, such as blessings (1983 CIC 1170), Catholic burial (1983 CIC 1183), weddings with nuptial Masses, and certain sacraments under certain conditions (1983 CIC 844). Hagedorn, pp. 83–84, does not directly hold that non-Catholic Christians are eligible for indulgences, but tends not to assume their eligibility for what seems to be light reasons and in any case for reasons suggested without the advantage of the insights of the Second Vatican Council (e.g., Vatican Council II, const. *Lumen gentium*, no. 8). Given the deeper post-conciliar appreciation of the elements of truth and charity contained within the Churches and ecclesial communities of baptized non-Catholics, it seems that, in regard to partial indulgences at least, one's "degree" of membership in the Church goes not to one's absolute eligibility to participate in indulgences, but rather to one's "disposition" (discussed later) for participation in indulgences; the closer one moves to the Church, of course, the more one is disposed for and eligible to participate in the fruits of the communion. In all of this, the growing phenomena of non-Catholics making use of devotions such as the Rosary, seeking sacramentals such as the reception of ashes on Ash Wednesday, and attending Sunday Mass frequently needs to be more fully appreciated.

want to be clear that any baptized person is basically eligible to obtain an indulgence. But because, as we shall see, one of the requirements for obtaining a *plenary* indulgence is going to sacramental Confession and receiving the Eucharist, non-Catholics are generally not able to obtain a plenary indulgence (1983 CIC 844).[13]

A member of the Christian faithful, properly disposed. This point on "proper disposition" is going to require a slightly longer explanation.[14] While baptism makes one generally *able* to receive an indulgence, disposition is what makes one *ready* to obtain a particular indulgence. The disposition required for indulgences varies somewhat, based on what kind of indulgence is desired. For accuracy's sake, we need to explain some important points about the disposition needed to obtain an indulgence.

Disposition for partial indulgences. In order to obtain a partial indulgence, one needs to be more than just baptized as stated above. Besides the specific requirements made by the indulgence itself (discussed later), one must be (1) not excommunicated (see immediately below), and (2) "in the state of grace," that is, one must be free of unforgiven mortal sins, at least by the end of the work required for the indulgence.[15] In this matter, one must avoid two perils: the first, "presumption" or a facile assumption that one is surely right with God, and the second, "scrupulosity," the unwarranted fear that one is gravely at odds with God (CCC 2092).[16] As a general rule, though, Christians who are

---

13. Though, even here, if, in accord with Canon 844, one who is a non-Catholic Christian becomes eligible to receive the Eucharist, does receive, and goes to sacramental Confession, then such a person would, in those two respects, be eligible to obtain even a plenary indulgence, including, of course, the plenary indulgence at the time of death.

14. Disposition is only briefly described in Enchiridion 1999, Norms 17 and 20, Enchiridion 1986, Norms 20 and 23, but the concept is essential for the proper understanding of indulgences.

15. Enchiridion 1999, Norm 17 § 1; Enchiridion 1986, Norm 20 § 1. See also de Angelis, nos. 59 and 119, and Hagedorn, pp. 86–88. Strictly speaking, one need only be in the state of grace at the conclusion of the work, and not through the entire period, to perform the work in question.

16. In the course of her trial, Joan of Arc was asked a loaded question: *Are you in the state of grace?* If Joan answered No, her judges would have an easy time building that admission into evidence of her guilt for other crimes, while if she answered Yes, she would be accused of hubris and conceit before God. Joan answered the question simply and brilliantly: "If I am in the state of grace," she said, "may God preserve me there. If I am not, may he speedily restore me to it." Trial of Joan of Arc, Rouen Testimony, Part III.

active in the practice of the faith[17] are more likely to be in "the state of grace" and, in that regard, are more able to benefit by indulgences.

Disposition for plenary indulgences. In order to obtain a plenary indulgence, there are some important requirements beyond those already listed.[18] These points require some elaboration. For a plenary indulgence, one must:

Not be excommunicated. Excommunication is the most severe, albeit medicinal, penalty that the Church has (CCC 1463; 1983 CIC 1311, 1331). The offenses for which excommunication can be imposed have been greatly reduced in recent decades.[19] Moreover, the process by which one might face excommunication is, today at least, designed so that as a practical matter, almost no one who might have faced formal excommunication in earlier times is in law excommunicated now.[20] For a variety of reasons, it is almost inconceivable that anyone who has not been formally notified of having been excommunicated (itself an extremely rare occurrence) is, as a matter of canon law, excommunicated.[21] Of course, the mere fact that one is not canonically excommunicated does *not* exclude the possibility that one might nevertheless, as the result of the activity that could have resulted in excommunication, be in the state of mortal sin, even if the canonical penalty of excommunication

---

17. One might consider in this regard the degree to which one adheres to the "Fundamental Precepts of the Church" outlined in CCC 2041–2043.

18. The conditions that are required for the acquisition of every plenary indulgence are known herein as "the usual conditions" and are discussed elsewhere. Note also that only one plenary indulgence may be gained in any given day (generally reckoned from midnight to midnight, 1983 CIC 202), while partial indulgences, on the other hand, may be gained as often as the underlying works are performed, other things being equal. See Enchiridion 1999, Norm 18 § 2; Enchiridion 1986, Norm 21, 2°. A few exceptions to these rules, discussed elsewhere, apply in the case of the indulgence at the time of death, under Enchiridion 1999, Norm 18, 2°; Enchiridion 1986, 21, 2°.

19. See 1983 CIC 1364 (apostasy, heresy, or schism); 1367 (sacrilege of the Eucharist); 1370 (physical attack on the pope); 1378 (certain other crimes in connection with sacraments); 1382 (unauthorized ordination of a bishop); 1388 (violation of the seal of confession); and 1398 (procuring abortion).

20. This is a complex area of canon law, but reading just 1983 CIC 1323–1324, 1341–1342, and 1347 will give one a sense as to how difficult, for better or worse, the process of enforcing any criminal law is in the Church just now, but especially a heavy sanction such as excommunication.

21. See 1983 CIC 1331 whereby formal notification of excommunication brings with it consequences beyond those associated with automatic excommunication.

is not in place. That sorry state could affect one's ability to obtain an indulgence because, as we saw above, one must be in the state of grace to obtain an indulgence.

Be inwardly contrite. The whole point of indulgences is to obtain, in full or in part, remission of the temporal penalty still owed for forgiven mortal and venial sins. Indulgences are, in other words, offered precisely to forgiven sinners who are sorry for having sinned. For indulgences to be most effective, a sinner conscious of having sins forgiven should renew that sorrow frequently and humbly, not in a way that suggests that the sins might not have been forgiven, but rather in a healthy way that expresses again the gratitude one feels to God the Father for having forgiven the sin, the gratitude that one feels to God the Son who paid the debt of our sins, and in gratitude to God the Holy Spirit who animates the life of grace in us toward our final union with God in heaven. Put another way, a forgiven sinner rejoices that he truly has been raised high above the filth of sin, but also understands that Christ did the heavy lifting!

One can establish one's sense of inward contrition in different ways. The first, and perhaps more salutary, way is by consciously renewing one's contrition when one is striving to obtain an indulgence. A few words, even mentally expressed, such as "Jesus, I am sorry for my sins" suffice. After a time, this practice becomes a virtuous and healthy habit, a regular part of one's daily life. Theologians refer to this as a "habitual" action, and habitual intentions, unless they are expressly revoked by the individual in word or deed, suffice for manifesting the contrition for sins necessary to obtain an indulgence.[22]

Have the intention to gain the indulgence. Indulgences are offered only to those who, among other things, *seek them*, that is, have the *intention of obtaining* them.[23] There are good reasons for this requirement, simple

---

22. Note that habitual intentions are recognized as being operative even before one forms what might in common parlance be called a habit. Yet another kind of intention, known as "inferred" or "presumed" or "virtual" intention, figures in the plenary indulgence offered at the time of death. We will discuss this kind of intention later.

23. In the special case of pursuing indulgences to be applied to the poor souls, the safer course, it seems, is to form the specific intention of gift deliberately, unless the indulgence is the kind that can only be gained for the dead (e.g., Enchiridion 1999, conc. 29). To strive for such a precious gift as an indulgence but to desire that it be applied to the benefit of another seems to call for a more deliberate expression of that choice. See also, Hagedorn, p. 99.

as it is to satisfy. Forming such an intention is a crucial way people have of *cooperating* with God in his salvific plan. Forming such an intention also brings one more consciously into a filial relation with the Church, the dispenser of indulgences, and helps us to "concretize" our relation with the Church. There are various ways to form the intention to obtain indulgences.

The easiest way to do this is simply to tell Our Lord, aloud or in one's mind, something like "Lord, I wish to gain every indulgence you ever offer me." If this sincere expression is never revoked, then it provides what theologians call a "habitual intention" and a habitual intention is sufficient in the matter of indulgences.[24]

Still, from time to time, even those enjoying the habitual intention to obtain an indulgence would be well advised to renew that intention, albeit simply and without fanfare. Renewing one's intention in this matter brings one into more frequent and conscious awareness that forgiveness of sin comes from God alone, and that we need his help to atone for our sins. For example, on one's birthday or on New Year's Day, one can tell Our Lord that one desires to obtain every indulgence so mercifully offered during the coming year. One might renew that intention with each liturgical season, say, on Ash Wednesday for the season of Lent, or when beginning more difficult work to which is attached a plenary indulgence (for example, a pilgrimage). Perhaps the best way of renewing one's habitual intention to obtain whatever indulgences are offered is to make such an intention part of the morning prayers that, however brief, should start the day of a every Christian.[25]

Perform the work. Looked at exteriorly, the effort required to obtain an indulgence, even a plenary indulgence, is minimal.[26] The days of enlisting in a crusade, fasting on bread and water for months, or walking barefoot to Rome are long gone. Today, it is quite clear that the difficult part of the indulgence is the interior conversion, the movement

---

24. Older Catholics who were likely taught as children to value indulgences and to seek them are likely to have expressed this desire to Our Lord and not to have revoked it (although they might have forgotten about it). Such a habitual intention would be sufficient for them to obtain indulgence many years later, though, as explained directly above, it is advisable to renew this intention from time to time. See also Hagedorn, pp. 93–94; de Angelis, no. 64.

25. Hagedorn, p. 94; de Angelis, n. 64.

26. "Come to Me all you who are weary . . . for my burden is easy, and my yoke is light." Matthew 11:28, 30.

ever genuinely deeper, ever closer, to Christ.[27] That's what requires grace and effort. Nevertheless, while no longer physically demanding, the works prescribed in the granting of an indulgence must still be undertaken and performed correctly. The "lightness" of the demand does not mean that it can be ignored.[28]

The performance of an indulgence is not a case of "magical rites" that yield effects simply upon the incantations being done in a precise way. Instead, the performance of the work in the way that the Church establishes they be done is an expression of solidarity with the whole Body of Christ and a willingness to show oneself humble before the authority that Christ himself gave to his Church. Moreover, since indulgences are a special favor and are not in any way due to us in justice, the Church can, and does, impose higher expectations in their execution than one might find in some areas of Church life. Finally, the Church has a long experience in the distribution of indulgences, and she has seen that laxity in their performance can, if unchecked, very easily lead to confusion about and even corruption of the indulgences by bringing them and the Church, their steward, into disrepute.

For these reasons, it is important to understand that one's ignorance of some requirement or other to obtain an indulgence, even where one's ignorance was "in good faith," does not excuse the failure to perform the work as directed.[29] An indulgence sought under these flawed circumstances either is not gained at all, or is obtained only in a diminished amount.

While most indulgences, whether plenary or partial, set forth various prayers or works to be undertaken as part of the indulgence, the acquisition of plenary indulgences requires that *additional* works and prayers, known as "the usual conditions," be performed. These additional requirements now need to be clearly set out. Briefly, they

---

27. "[I]ndulgences cannot be gained without genuine conversion (*metanoia*) and union with God, to which the performance of prescribed works is attached." *Doctrina*, no. 11.

28. It need hardly be added that one must perform the works personally. The only exception that older authors admitted was when it came to distributing alms, in which case an agent could perform the actual distribution of gifts made by the one seeking the indulgence. De Angelis, no. 67; Hagedorn, p. 109.

29. Hagedorn, pp. 106–107.

are three: sacramental Confession, Eucharistic communion, and prayer for the pope's intention.[30]

Sacramental confession means just that, going to the Sacrament of Reconciliation. An act of perfect contrition, while obviously praiseworthy and effective against the liability of guilt for sin, does not satisfy the requirement of sacramental Confession that is necessary for the gaining of a plenary indulgence. A single sacramental Confession, however, carried out "several days before or after" the prayers or works required for the indulgence(s) in question, suffices for application to several plenary indulgences.[31]

Eucharistic communion must be by physical reception of the sacrament.[32] This reception is expressly encouraged to take place on the same day the prayers or works associated with the indulgence in question are performed, but as with Confession, the reception of Communion can take place several days before or after those undertakings.[33] Unlike

---

30. Enchiridion 1999, Norm 20; Enchiridion 1986, Norm 23. See also Hagedorn, pp. 119–127; de Angelis 72–96. Among "the usual conditions" in times past was, very frequently, a visitation to a church or oratory. See Hagedorn, pp. 128–129 and de Angelis, nos. 82–84. This is no longer a "usual condition" for the gaining of indulgences in general and is required only for specific indulgences calling for such a visit. Older discussions as to what kind of sacred edifice sufficed for what kind of indulgence have thus largely been mooted. Where an indulgence does call for activities within a church and oratory, one may consult canon law (1983 CIC 1214–1229) for descriptions of these sacred edifices, but in brief, almost anything that is not a private chapel in a private residence qualifies as a church or oratory for purposes of this indulgence.

31. Older norms required these additional actions to be undertaken within the octave of the main work. See 1917 CIC 931 § 1 and Hagedorn, pp. 122–123. Such specific norms are no longer in force, but they might provide a useful guide to those who wonder at what point the unity of the actions that go into a plenary indulgence might be threatened. Note that on January 29, 2000, William Cardinal Baum, Major Penitentiary of the Apostolic Penitentiary, published a letter "The Gift of the Indulgence" in which he determined that a sacramental Confession "within several (about 20) days before or after" the performance of the requirements for an indulgence satisfied the Confession requirement for the indulgence. English text available on the Vatican Web site (www.vatican.va), see Apostolic Penitentiary. Confirmed by letter to Dr. Peters, March 18, 2005. This same time period may be used for determining the period within which Holy Communion may be taken for purposes of a plenary indulgence. As a practical matter, then, the practice of monthly Confession allows one to benefit from plenary indulgences at all times, as one would always be within 20 days, before or after, a sacramental Confession made once a month.

32. "Spiritual Communion," while praiseworthy in itself, does not suffice for this reception requirement, and the Communion must not be sacrilegious, that is, Communion must be received by one in the state of grace. CCC 1385, 1415; 1983 CIC 916. See also Hagedorn, p. 126.

33. Older norms allowed this reception of Communion to take place not earlier than noon of the day preceding the performance of the indulgence, and not later than eight days following its completion. See 1917 CIC 931 § 1, and Hagedorn, p. 126, and De Angelis, no. 77. But see footnote above in regard to Cardinal Baum's letter of January 29, 2000, wherein the period for

Confession, however, a single reception of the Eucharist can be applied only to a single plenary indulgence.[34]

Prayers for the pope's intentions imply not so much prayers for the welfare of his person, but for the intentions that he holds closest to his heart as pope.[35] One need not articulate these intentions, or even be aware of what they might specifically be at that time; general prayer for his intentions suffices. These prayers may be left to the ingenuity of the faithful, but the requirement can be satisfied with an *Our Father* and a *Hail Mary*.[36] Again, it is expressly encouraged that one offer the prayers for the pope on the same day the prayers or works associated with the indulgence in question are performed but, as with Confession and reception of the Eucharist, the offering of prayers for the pope can take place several days before or after those undertakings. Moreover, one's prayers for the pope's intention can be applied only to a single plenary indulgence. Particular postures in prayer are not required.[37]

Notwithstanding this "strict construction" approach that the Church orders in the matter of indulgences, the Church herself, from

---

reception of Communion was set about 20 days, before or after the performance of the indulgenced work. Also, under certain circumstances, one may licitly receive Holy Communion twice on a given day (see 1983 CIC 917). Thus, although one is generally limited to one plenary indulgence per day, one could nevertheless apply a second reception of the Eucharist on a given day toward a plenary indulgence otherwise striven for up to 20 days before or after the reception of the second Eucharist.

34. Although few Catholics active in their faith limit themselves to but a single annual reception of the Eucharist (the minimum set down by 1983 CIC 920), the so-called Easter duty Communion, even though it is an act required by law, would satisfy the reception of Communion requirement for a plenary indulgence. See de Angelis, no. 78, and Hagedorn, pp. 103, 127.

35. See generally Hagedorn p. 119, who cites such papal intentions as welfare of the Church, conversion of sinners, and so forth. The prayers for the pope offered during services and liturgies that one is not otherwise required to attend (for example, the intercessions offered during the Veneration of Cross on Good Friday) would also seem to suffice as prayers for the pope's intention. Also, during the interregnum period between papacies, prayers for what would technically be the last pope's intentions certainly suffice. Keep in mind, as Abp. Dolan noted in his foreword to this book, that the Apostolic Penitentiary itself, the dicastery charged with the administration of indulgences, remains fully functional during the interim period between papacies, as the "gates of mercy" are never closed.

36. There is here, in other words, not the typical requirement that such prayers be taken from a formally approved text. Spontaneous or extemporaneous prayers are acceptable here. Note, however, that as these prayers are intended to serve the needs of the pope, they may not be used to satisfy other prayer requirements that might be laid down in specific situations. For example, the *Our Father* required in connection with the visitation of church and the *Our Father* for the pope's intention, serving distinct ends, must be prayed separately.

37. De Angelis, no. 94; Hagedorn, p. 114.

time to time, in the granting of the indulgence itself, makes allowance for the impossibility of performing certain parts of the work.[38] In such cases, one who is truly impeded from performing the work as presented in the grant can take advantage of whatever allowance for difficulty or impossibility is contained in the grant itself. Of course, if a given indulgence sets various options before the faithful, one can freely choose among them in accord with one's circumstances.[39]

Finally, confessors (whether in the celebration of Reconciliation or outside it) are empowered under certain circumstances to commute or modify certain works necessary to obtain to indulgences for the pastoral benefit of the individual(s) seeking an indulgence.[40] At times, these modification, or commutations, can be significant.[41] In these kinds of situations, though, it is important to understand that it is the confessor's decision, not the desires or wishes of the faithful, that controls.[42]

---

38. An example here would be Enchiridion 1999, Norm 25, by which local ordinaries and hierarchs may authorize the reception of plenary indulgences without sacramental Confession or Communion by those who cannot satisfy those conditions without great hardship. Instead, such persons may express their contrition interiorly and resolve to receive these sacraments as soon as possible. Note that the phrase "local ordinary" includes more diocesan officials than simply the diocesan bishop (1983 CIC 134). Moreover, Enchiridion 1999, Norm 26, makes special provision for the deaf and mute by enabling them to obtain indulgences under modified circumstances made necessary by their physical conditions. On other accommodations for the deaf and mute in pre-conciliar indulgences, see Raccolta, no. 772.

39. An example here would be the options granted for reciting either version of the ancient Creed, picking among various Litanies, or using different ways of praying the Rosary. In an even more striking way, the alternative means of satisfying the requirements for the Stations of the Cross or the Divine Mercy Sunday indulgence (both discussed elsewhere) are a clear demonstration of the Church's desire to mitigate the effects of impossibility or serious inconvenience in the acquisition of indulgences.

40. Enchiridion 1999, Norm 24; Enchiridion 1986, Norm 27.

41. See, e.g., Hagedorn, p. 108, on the legitimate commutation of a former indulgence that required fifteen visits to Basilicas to just three visits. Accommodations for the sick could also be considered in this regard.

42. A special case here, one not dependent on a confessor's decision, concerns the acquisition of indulgences by deaf, speech-impaired, or handicapped persons. For the first two groups, Enchiridion 1999, Norm 26, makes express provision: indulgences are available to these persons who raise their minds to God or who join mentally in the public prayers associated with indulgences, while as for private prayers, it suffices to read them silently or express them in sign language. For the handicapped who are unable to render some of the gestures associated with indulgences (e.g., the Sign of the Cross because of paralysis or amputation) it suffices that they make what gesture they can, if any, while offering the prayers. *Canon Law Digest* I: 423. These accommodations do not require a confessor's mediation, because they are already set forth in the norms themselves, or are evident from the principle that no one is bound to the impossible. See also de Angelis, no. 94.

Be free of any attachment to sin. We have come now to the discussion
of the most difficult requirement for the proper disposition necessary
for the acquisition of plenary indulgence, namely, the requirement that
one be free from all attachment to sin.[43] This requirement, more than
all of the others combined, is what makes obtaining a plenary indulgence so difficult.[44]

It may understandably be remarked that, given the enormity
of sin, most of the works that count toward plenary indulgences (say,
recitation of a rosary or a half hour in front of the Blessed Sacrament)
seem a very small price to pay to escape the punishment that one
would otherwise undergo for such offenses. But from this incomplete
perception of the norms on indulgences, two errors could emerge:
first, that maybe sin is not so terrible after all, if its punishments can
be completely ameliorated by such small acts; and second, that maybe
these small acts must be performed with some kind of superhuman
attention to detail, as if an extravagance of piety were necessary for a
plenary indulgence. Both of these errors overlook a crucial requirement
for one seeking a plenary indulgence. Admittedly, this requirement,
while latent in earlier prescription on indulgences,[45] has only emerged
clearly with the post-conciliar reforms of Pope Paul VI.

Freedom from attachment to sin means more than just commit-
ment to avoid *committing* sins. That is a start, of course, but not the end
of one's effort to exclude sin from one's life. Freedom from attachment
to sin means more; it means freedom from any *affection* for sin,
elimination of fondness for sin (even in memory), exclusion of any
openness to sin under certain conditions.[46] It means a wholesome fear

---

43. Enchiridion 1999, Norm 20 § 1; Enchiridion 1986, Norm 23, 1°.

44. For what *is* acquired by those striving for, but failing to obtain for any reason, a plenary
indulgence, namely, a partial indulgence, see Enchiridion 1999, Norm 20 § 4; Enchiridion
1986, Norm 23, 4°.

45. Consider Hagedorn, writing in 1924, at p. 65: "The gaining of a plenary indulgence as
such is not an easy matter."

46. Saint Francis de Sales discusses affection for venial sin, and the necessity of banishing
it from the soul, in his *Introduction to the Devout Life*, Part I, chap. 22: " . . . You will find
then, my child, that besides the mortal sins and their affections from which your soul has
already been purged, you are beset by sundry inclinations and tendencies to venial sin; mind,
I do not say you will find venial sins, but the inclination and tendency to them. Now, one is
quite different from the other. We can never be altogether free from venial sin, at least not
until after a very long persistence in this purity; but we can be without any affection for venial
sin. It is altogether one thing to have said something unimportant [that is] not strictly true,
out of carelessness or liveliness, and quite a different matter to take pleasure in lying, and in

of the Lord, lest one fall into one's old ways again. Outside of special favors from God, freedom from attachment to or affection for sin does not come easily or quickly.

One who is free from any attachment to sin is not (again, except in the case of very special favors from God) free of temptation to sin. Temptations still arise, but they are banished immediately, without a second's hesitation or regret. One who is free from attachment to sin might in actuality still commit venial sins, but these sins are immediately repented of and the weakness that is thus exposed is promptly addressed.[47] At an intellectual level, a Christian might recognize that freedom from attachment to sin is to be desired as quickly as possible, but that one has not yet arrived at that point and, in all honesty, is quite far from it. Strive on, knowing that Christ's help will not be lacking.

With that extended but necessary discussion of "proper disposition" needed for obtaining indulgences behind us, we can now return to our explanation of the definition of an indulgence.

A member of the Christian faithful, properly disposed, obtains. Obviously, "to obtain" means to get or acquire, but the Church also wants us to know that we can enjoy a *certainty* about the fact of having obtained an indulgence if we fulfill the requirements for one. De Angelis put it this way: "The works that are laid down by ecclesiastical power for securing an indulgence are considered conditions that, once fulfilled, yield effects. An indulgence for the living, therefore, works *ex opere operato* in that, if the conditions are carefully fulfilled, the

---

the habitual practice thereof. But I tell you that you must purify your soul from all inclination to venial sin; that is to say, you must not voluntarily retain any deliberate intention of permitting yourself to commit any venial sin whatever. It would be most unworthy consciously to admit anything so displeasing to God, as the will to offend Him in anywise. Venial sin, however small, is displeasing to God, although it be not so displeasing as the greater sins which involve eternal condemnation; and if venial sin is displeasing to Him, any clinging which we tolerate to mortal sin is nothing less than a resolution to offend His Divine Majesty. Is it really possible that a rightly disposed soul can not only offend God, but take pleasure therein?" Rivingstons trans., 1876. See also de Angelis, no. 10.

47. One with unforgiven venial sin on one's soul cannot obtain a plenary indulgence, particularly where the presence of venial sin suggests any lingering attachment to sin. Hagedorn, p. 65. Given, as noted earlier, the many ways a Christian has of seeking and receiving forgiveness for venial sins, however, one setting about the works prescribed for a plenary indulgence should not fail to seek such forgiveness at the outset of this work.

effect of the indulgence is, as we have said, infallible."[48] Again, the extremes of presumption and scrupulosity must be avoided.

Obtains under certain and definite conditions. Christ entrusted the treasury of his merits to the Church and granted her the authority to set out the conditions upon which they are applied.[49] There are, of course, many ways that we can show God our love, our sorrow for having offended him, and our desire to be one with him. All of these are acceptable to God, all of them give us a share in the merits of Jesus Christ. But if we want that *additional* share in those merits offered to us by way of indulgences, it is appropriate, and necessary, that we observe the laws laid down by the Church for their acquisition. In many ways, of course, those rules and conditions are, as we shall see, easy to satisfy, but satisfied they must be. These conditions can and have varied over time. It is a settled matter, though, that once the conditions are laid down by the Church, they are to be strictly interpreted, with exceptions being very few and clearly outlined. Ignorance or even mistakes made in good faith while pursuing an indulgence do not excuse the failure to comply with the terms of the grant.[50] In this book, we will identify some exceptions to the fulfillment of conditions that are allowed. Recall that one of the fundamental notions underlying indulgences is the ability of one Christian in the Church to assist another. Were one to disregard the laws of the Church in attempting to share in the treasures of the Church, one would hardly be acting consistently with the demands of that communion upon which we are drawing such benefits.

---

48. De Angelis, no. 12.

49. See Christ's broad commissioning of Saint Peter as recorded in Matthew 18: 15–18.

50. For some (perhaps dated) examples of modifications in litanies that were held to have deprived their users of the indulgences attached thereto, see *Canon Law Digest* I: 451. Even here, though, prudence is required. A very old principle of canon law is relevant here: "Favors are to be amplified", or in Latin, "*favores ampliari.*" See Regulae Iuris Bonifacii VIII, in *Libro Sexto Corporis Iuris Canonici* (1298), no. 15. For example, if, in the public recitation of the Rosary, the leader inadvertently omits one of the Hail Marys from a decade, there is no obligation to go back and add it privately. If one recites a litany, and later discovers that an invocation was left out, one still obtains whatever indulgence was attached to the recitation, though one would certainly have to amend the list for the future use. See Hagedorn, pp. 106–107. Similarly, if, for example, an indulgence is made available to those watching a live event on television or listening to it on the radio, it seems, *favores ampliari*, reasonable to conclude that such indulgence is also obtained by those following the event live on the Internet by a "Web cast" even though that option is not expressly mentioned in the grant. In general, issues related to the substantive requirements of an indulgence, as opposed to the method of performing those requirements, are more significant and therefore admit of less variation or alternative fulfillment.

Note in this regard that some indulgences are tied to liturgical celebrations held on certain days.[51] Whenever the celebration of that day has been transferred to another day by legitimate ecclesiastical authority, the indulgence offered for that day transfers as well.[52]

By action of the Church that as minister of redemption dispenses and authoritatively applies. These phrases simply underscore a point already made, namely, that the Church has been given charge over the treasury of merits won by Christ.[53] Implicit here is the idea that the Church is not the cause of our redemption but rather its minister. Moreover, the treasures of the Church, even its spiritual ones, are not to be hoarded away, but rather are to be actively disseminated so that as many people as possible can benefit from the infinite merits of Christ. Today this authority is exercised chiefly through the Apostolic Penitentiary, a dicastery of the Roman Curia that has special care for matters related to conscience.[54]

The treasury of the satisfactions of Christ and the saints. Paul VI banished any misunderstanding that "The Treasury of the Church" was to be found in her material possessions which can be, at times, very impressive.[55] Rather, the inexhaustible treasury of the Church is Jesus Christ himself, the infinite merit he has in the Father's eyes, and the boundless love and mercy he offers for our salvation. At no time, and in no way, can the satisfactions that Christ won on Calvary ever be diminished, let alone used up. Indeed, the spiritual treasury of the Church is still growing.[56]

The same God who allows human beings to share in his creative power over the universe, who allows sinners to become his

---

51. See, e.g. Enchiridion 1999, conc. 7 §1, 3° (*Corpus Christi*) or conc. 21 (Prayers in honor of Saints and Blesseds).

52. Enchiridion 1999, Norm 13; Enchiridion 1986, Norm 16.

53. Enchiridion 1999, Norm 5; Enchiridion 1986, Norm 7. See also CCC 1478, and 1983 CIC 995.

54. Enchiridion 1999, Norm 6; Enchiridion 1986, Norm 8. The Congregation for the Doctrine of the Faith works closely with the Apostolic Penitentiary regarding aspects of indulgences that have some impact on Catholic doctrine. For brief descriptions of which Holy See offices historically had authority over indulgences, see Hagedorn, pp. 78–79 and de Angelis, no. 33.

55. *Doctrina*, 5. Recall also Saint Peter's words in Acts (3:6): "Silver and gold I have not, but I give you what I have."

56. For more on the Communion of Saints in the context of indulgences, see, e.g., de Angelis, nos. 4–9 and Hagedorn, pp. 52–55.

representatives and ministers in the world, and who gives us the strength to share in his sufferings borne for our salvation, also, in no less incredible a way, allows the baptized to make contributions to The Treasury of the Church, and has arranged it so that their small but real contributions can be used for our spiritual benefit.

In the first place, of course, among creatures contributing to the spiritual treasury of the Church stands the Blessed Virgin Mary, Mother of God and Queen of the Universe, whose prayers and good works please God beyond those of any other human being.[57] Having remained, by her cooperation with a singular grace of God, sinless her whole life (CCC 411, 490), Mary pours her vast love into the treasury of the Church. But with her are also all the saints (formally recognized and otherwise) who strove to unite their lives with Christ's and who pleased God not only by willingly accepting the token punishments that they owed for their sins, but then in bursts of love and self-sacrifice, added their own merits, however small compared to Christ's and albeit won with Christ's help, into the treasury in such a way that, as Paul VI noted, that treasury continues to grow with each passing day.[58] Of course, these human contributions differ from those of Christ in that the Lord needs no help in making his contribution to the treasury of merits, whereas human beings can make additions only with his help. Nevertheless, these contributions, however small they are in comparison with Christ's, are real, and they are of real help to sinners in repairing the damages their sins have caused.

This completes our basic examination of what an indulgence is, but some important questions about indulgences are not yet answered, or at least are not answered in depth, by just looking at the definition of an indulgence. Recalling that, as a rule, the more one understands about indulgences, the better one is able to pursue them, let us take a look at some of the more common questions that remain about indulgences.

---

57. *Doctrina*, 5.
58. *Doctrina*, 5.

Chapter 4

Other Important Aspects of Indulgences

Some important questions on indulgences remain to be treated. They are grouped here for convenience. These questions cannot be readily or fully answered by looking only at the definition of an indulgence, and instead depend more heavily on the explorations of commentators over the centuries. Remember, as always, that one need not master these finer points in order to benefit by indulgences, but that a better understanding of these topics can be an incentive to make more active use of the gift of indulgences.

WHO MAY BENEFIT BY AN INDULGENCE?

Theoretically, three categories of persons can benefit by any given indulgence won by a specific Christian. Those three are: (1) The Christian person himself, (2) Other living members of the Christian faithful, or (3) the faithful departed in Purgatory.[1] Examples of indulgences operating in all three ways are found throughout Church history. Current ecclesiastical law, however, allows indulgences to be applied only for two of these groups, namely, for the Christian himself, and for the faithful departed.[2] (See table 4.1.)

In principle, there is no reason why indulgences won by one member of the faithful cannot be applied to another living member.[3] After all, the words of Saint Paul and the earliest expressions of what

---

1. Indulgences cannot benefit those in Hell (for they are beyond help) or those in Heaven (for they have no need of help). See Hagedorn, p. 96.

2. Enchiridion 1999, Norm 3; Enchiridion 1986, Norms 3 and 4.

3. Hagedorn, at pp. 97–98, observes that such a benefit, while theoretically possible, would be outside of anything in ecclesiastical tradition.

Table 4.1   Possible Beneficiaries of Indulgences

The Individual Actor	Other Living Members of the Faithful	The Faithful Departed
Obtained certainly by the individual when performed in accord with Church discipline	Not currently allowed	Applied to the dead by way of "suffrage" or prayer

later developed into the doctrine of indulgences bear witness to the idea that one member of the Church on earth can and ought to share another's burdens (Galatians 6:2). But it is the pastoral judgment of the Church *today* that extending the benefits of an indulgence won by one member of the faithful to another living member of the faithful would work to the recipient's disadvantage, perhaps by removing an incentive to engage personally in the dispositions, works, and prayers called for by indulgences in the first place.[4] Then again, to allow the practice of applying indulgences to other living members of the Church (specifically, those who could and should be making use of the sacraments and sacramental themselves) might lead some to think that indulgences can be obtained without first seeking forgiveness for the guilt of the underlying sins. In any case, the Church, as steward of the merits won by Christ on the Cross, has the authority to make these determinations and has exercised that authority.

Because an indulgence is the application, not of our merits, but rather of the infinite merits of Jesus Christ (to which are added over time the merits of the saints) and is made in accord with the discipline of his Church on earth, we can, as we have seen, know with certainty that an indulgence obtained by those seeking it is accepted by God in full or partial remission of our debt of sin, as the case may be. In this regard, indulgences might be said to resemble the actions of sacraments, in that they may be seen to operate *ex opere operato*, that is, in virtue of the action being performed.[5] While the *amount* of punishment forgiven for a specific individual obtaining a plenary indulgence, or the *amount* of punishment forgiven for a specific individual obtaining a partial indulgence, cannot be known with certainty (because only God knows specifically how much sin is affront to himself, as explained

---

4. See Hagedorn, p. 97.
5. De Angelis, no. 12.

below), the fact of some amount of due punishment having been remitted *can* be known with certainty by the one performing the action and applying it to himself.

As for indulgences obtained by a living member of the faithful and applied to the poor souls in purgatory, however, the manner of our certainty about its application is somewhat different. Here it must be recalled that the authority of Church, as granted by Christ, extends only to its members living here on earth. What is known as "the power of the keys"[6] does not extend to the souls in purgatory (and even less to those with God in Heaven!). So, while the Church can, with Christ's own authority, apply the merits of Christ to her members living here on earth with certainty as to their effect, it can present those same shares in Christ's merits known as indulgences to the souls in purgatory not "by way of jurisdiction," but only by way of prayer or request, or technically, "suffrage."[7] To be sure, the prayers by which indulgences are offered on behalf of the poor souls are the prayers of Christ's Church, and they represent our efforts to share the love of God with our departed brothers and sisters; as such, one can be confident that such indulgences are received by God and applied in the most beneficial way according to his wisdom.[8] It is not for us to have specific certainty about the precise result of those indulgences, but only to have the confidence that we are doing what God wants us to do as best we know how to do it.[9] None of this should in any way discourage the seeking of indulgences on behalf of the faithful departed, including persons specifically identified in our intentions. It does serve to caution us against overly facile conclusions that a specific result is obtained when, in truth, the Church does not claim that degree of authority or knowledge.[10]

---

6. Matthew 16: 18–19 and 18: 18. See also Hagedorn, pp. 57–58.

7. Hagedorn, pp. 58–61.

8. This also supports the idea that indulgences offered for the dead are of greater efficacy, all other things being equal, than is mere intercession on their behalf, for personal prayer, while good, does not enjoy the preeminence associated with the prayers and actions of the whole Church as is the case with indulgences. See Hagedorn, pp. 59–60.

9. Other interesting questions, but questions on which the Church has taken no position, come to mind here: for example, if more indulgences are offered for a soul in purgatory than that soul needs, what happens to those not needed, as it were? Was it already included in God's providence, or is it applied to the needs of other suffering souls, and if so, in what way?

10. Concluding too quickly, for example, that one has succeeded in obtaining a plenary indulgence, and then that one has actually applied that indulgence for a specific soul in

What Does an Indulgence Accomplish?

It is natural to ask, more precisely, what does an indulgence accomplish? or, in other words, "how much it is worth?" Such questions do not imply that one has a "calculating spirit" toward God, for anyone who sincerely asks these questions should already understand that indulgences are a gift from Christ more to be treasured than reckoned. In any case, to such questions the Church has quite reasonable answers.

Over the course of the centuries, there have been various ways of assessing the worth of indulgences, especially of those we would call today "partial" indulgences. Under some quite early systems, partial indulgences were reckoned to remit one-half, or one-third, or one-fourth of one's liability of punishment for sins already forgiven. Notice that under such a system, the same action performed by different persons could result in significantly different amounts of remission of punishment depending on the amount or depth of the debt of punishment that was owed for forgiven sins in the first place. This "percentage of punishment" system is no longer in place.

Later indulgence systems remitted specific periods of penance, (say an indulgence that remitted the equivalent of four weeks of fasting, or two months worth of vigils, and so on). Over time, this indulgence system eventually evolved into the one that, today, older Catholics might still recall, that is, one wherein indulgences were measured in so many days or years. Unfortunately, this system lent itself to many misunderstandings. People had long lost appreciation of the length and severity of older penances, and without them as a model, they sought to explain the measurement of indulgences as time remitted from purgatorial suffering. That was not an unreasonable guess, but it assumed vastly more specificity about purgatorial sufferings than the Church has ever asserted,[11] including whether it can even be measured in time at all. Moreover, among those who had some understanding of the time periods applied under older penitential disciplines, when they saw how much penance was believed to be remitted by the light deeds

---

Purgatory, might result in the cessation of further prayers or sacrifices for that person who, in reality, still stood to benefit by such spiritual gifts.

11. For an overview of the complexities and uncertainties about certain aspects of Purgatory, including its "duration" and "intensity," see Bastien, esp. p. 1036.

required for most partial indulgences, there was an inevitable tendency to hold indulgences cheap.

All of these misconceptions and bases for misunderstanding, however, have been removed by Pope Paul VI in *Doctrina* and by the consequent legislation on indulgences. To see how clear and balanced the new assessment of indulgences now is, let us look at plenary and partial indulgences separately.

A Plenary Indulgence

While earning a plenary indulgence is, and is meant to be, relatively difficult,[12] it is easy to determine its value to a living person: quite simply, a plenary indulgence accounts for *all* of the liability of punishment owed by one for forgiven sins up to that time.[13] God alone knows exactly how much punishment, in absolute terms, would have been due for the forgiven sins of a specific person, but whatever the amount of that punishment was, God accepts the indulgence as payment in full, or, more precisely, he accepts the application of the infinite merits of Christ from the treasury of his Church to pay the debt of punishment of the forgiven sinner who obtains a plenary indulgence.[14]

Those striving for a plenary indulgence, given its difficulty and occasional complexity, might fail to obtain it. In these cases, however, they do not walk away empty-handed, as if God took no note of their efforts to love him all the more by striving to obtain an indulgence. Rather, in such cases, these persons may achieve a partial indulgence.[15] There is, admittedly, a great difference between having all of one's liability for punishment being paid by an indulgence, and having only part of that liability remitted, and this in turn could lead to some discouragement among those seeking a plenary indulgence when, it seems, one might only to achieve a partial. But one must be careful about appreciating, accurately enough, the difficulty of attaining

---

12. *Doctrina*, 12; Hagedorn, p. 65.

13. Enchiridion 1999, Norm 2; Enchiridion 1986, Norm 2.

14. In this regard, obviously, not all plenary indulgences are equal in the "amount" of the debt they remit. One forgiven sinner might have an enormous liability of punishment due for those sins, while another sinner might have in comparison just a small amount. A plenary indulgence would pay each debt in full, regardless of the "absolute amount" of punishment due in God's eyes.

15. Enchiridion 1999, Norm 20 § 4; Enchiridion 1986, Norm 23 § 4.

plenary indulgences, and then concluding, quite inaccurately, that they
are not worth striving for in the practical order. The Church offers no
insight as to how much of one's punishment God remits in the case
of those striving for, but failing to obtain, a plenary indulgence, except
to say that whatever the remission is will be "partial." Still, to use a
mathematical analogy, suppose God remits only one per cent of the
punishment owed because of sin. Even that would be well worth
striving for. But, as we also know, God will not be outdone in generosity.
For all we know, God might remit, to continue the numerical analogy,
not just one per cent our punishments if we fail to obtain a plenary
indulgence, and not even just ten per cent, but ninety-nine percent of
the punishment that we still owe for our forgiven sins! The difficulty
of obtaining plenary indulgences is real, but the benefit for striving
for them is just as real and should help to keep us from becoming
discouraged in the face of their requirements.

A Partial Indulgence

Earning a partial indulgence is, and is meant to be, relatively easy, but
determining its precise benefit to an individual is a more complicated.
Beyond simply saying that a partial indulgence remits "part" of the
punishment owed for sin,[16] three factors determine the worth of any
given action as performed by any given person, and these same factors
are now used by the Church to determine the value of a particular
partial indulgence undertaken by a member of the faithful. Those three
factors are (1) The nature of the action undertaken, (2) The degree
of perfection with which the action is performed, and (3) The holiness
of the individual performing the action. Let's open them up and then
discuss them (see Table 4.2).

This analysis, of course, can be applied to any action undertaken
out of love for God, regardless of whether one is also seeking to obtain
an indulgence thereby. There are many Christians who undertake
actions, whether of penance or of charity, without advertence to the
possibility of gaining an indulgence. These actions are seen by God as
good and are acceptable to him in accord with their intrinsic merits.[17]

---

16. Enchiridion 1999, Norm 2; Enchiridion 1986, Norm 2.

17. Put another way, one should hardly regret having done something for God without
having sought an indulgence for them at the same time. Acts of repentance and love are always

Table 4.2   Partial Indulgences

The Action Undertaken		The Actor performing the Work or Prayer
Nature the Action	Perfection of the Action	Holiness of the Doer
Only God knows the precise worth of any particular action, but, broadly speaking, some actions are clearly nobler or more significant than others. Actions that demand more effort on our part are generally of more benefit to ourselves, and are rewarded in greater measure by God.	Identical actions can be performed with different degrees of "perfection." An action that is performed with greater care, attention, and completeness is generally of more benefit to oneself and is rewarded more richly by God than are actions that are sloppily, inattentively, or incompletely undertaken.[18]	Only God knows the degree of holiness enjoyed by any specific person at any given time, but in general the efforts of those who are closer to him in the life of grace are more pleasing to him than are those of others who are yet farther off from him.[19]

Nevertheless, the Church in accord with ancient traditions also makes available indulgences from its inexhaustible spiritual treasury for certain prayers and actions undertaken with conscious advertence to the gift of indulgences. Today, instead of trying to express the value of that gift as a "percentage of punishment remitted" or "time of penance remitted," the value of the indulgence that the Church adds to the prayers or actions undertaken by a member of the faithful is, quite simply, equal to that worth.[20] In other words, the Church matches what we offer to Christ (albeit with his help) with another equivalent share in the merits of Christ that he left to his Church's disposal. In the simplest terms, by making use of indulgences, a suitably disposed member of the faithful effectively doubles one's gift

pleasing to God in and of themselves, and we should always be glad that we had the grace and opportunity to perform them.

18. Even the same individual performing the same act at different times might perform the action with more attention and care at one time than at another.

19. Note that, in a way that might seem ironic at first, this understanding of disposition implies that those who need indulgences less (because they are already closer to God because of their love for him) actually benefit more by indulgences than those who need their relief in greater degree. This should not be seen as unfair, of course, or backwards, but rather, serve as a greater spur for the rest of us to move as close to God as possible, knowing that he will never be outdone in love or generosity.

20. Enchiridion 1999, Norm 4; Enchiridion 1986, Norm 5; *Doctrina*, 12.

to God, by asking him to double his gift to us! The atonement one makes toward the liability of punishment owed for forgiven sins is doubled by making use of the indulgence that might be attached to those prayers and actions.

A Closer Look at Some Other Norms on Indulgences

While several of the introductory norms on indulgences have already been discussed, some warrant additional attention here.

Non-Papal Authority over Indulgences

Authority over indulgences primarily belongs to the Roman Pontiff, and that authority can be and is often delegated to others under certain conditions.[21] If the current restrictions on this authority to establish indulgences seem severe, one must recall what a terrible price the Church paid in the past for abuses in the indulgence system, and understand her reluctance to allow conditions like those to arise again.[22]

At present, basically no one below the rank of bishop or eparch has authority to establish indulgences.[23] These officers, however, have considerable authority in the establishment of indulgences, albeit partial ones.[24] Moreover, these also have the authority to impart an

---

21. Enchiridion 1999, Norms 5–11; Enchiridion 1986, Norms 8–13.

22. Hagedorn, p. 73. Admittedly, some of the worst abuses, including those that in part triggered Luther's reactions, occurred under indulgences authorized, but poorly supervised, by Rome. Unfortunately, while such abuses are all too well remembered, the great good that sprang up in the wake of some indulgences goes forgotten. See, e.g., P. Palmer, "Indulgences" *New Catholic Encyclopedia* (New York: McGraw-Hill, 1967), vol. 7: 482–484, at p. 484.

23. There is no intrinsic reason why inferior prelates, and even those not in holy orders, may not establish indulgences, but the further "down the list" one goes, the less historical precedent one finds for such exercises. See Hagedorn, p. 75. Strictly speaking, though, because authority to establish partial indulgences has been extended to "those equivalent in law" to diocesan bishops and eparchs, and because priests set over certain other groupings of the faithful are in that class (see 1983 CIC 134, 368–371), at least some priests could have the authority to establish partial indulgences under the current law.

24. Enchiridion 1999, Norm 7, 1° (clarifying earlier norms that all those present in a bishop's or eparch's territory, as well as their subjects outside of it, may benefit from such indulgences); Enchiridion 1986, Norm 10, 1°. It seems that this rather wide authority to establish partial indulgences has not been exercised by many diocesan bishops or eparchs. This might be explained by the fact that Specific Grant indulgences offered in the Enchiridion are themselves the most popular already, and that the introduction of General Grant indulgences eliminates the need for much supplementation at the local level. On the other hand, surely some ecclesiastical

apostolic blessing, to which a plenary indulgence is attached,[25] three times per year at special liturgical functions at which they celebrate or preside.[26] These opportunities for the plenary indulgence at such liturgies must be announced beforehand. The blessing that bishops and eparchs customarily give, for example, as they process out at the end of Mass is not the papal blessing described here.

In like manner, metropolitans (1983 CIC 435), whom Latin-rite Catholics usually call "archbishops," have authority to establish partial indulgences in their suffragan sees as well as in their own, but not to impart the apostolic blessing outside of their own archdioceses.[27] Finally, cardinals may grant partial indulgences, but only for particular occasions and then only to be gained by those in attendance.[28]

In all cases wherein authorities below the level of the Roman Pontiff wish to establish (partial) indulgences for all the faithful under their authority, they are required to give advance notice of the same to the Holy See.[29] This represents a tightening of the earlier norm that only required that *notice* of partial indulgences eventually be sent to the Holy See under pain of nullification of the grant—a consequence that could have caused confusion and hardship to the faithful striving for such indulgences but who, through no fault of their own, might have lost the benefits they thought they had acquired. The current restriction does not apply to plenary indulgences offered by way of the apostolic blessing (because this indulgence is not established by the

---

undertakings in particular Churches would be fostered by making wider use of the authority granted.

25. See Enchiridion 1999, Norms 7 and 9; Enchiridion 1986, Norms 10, 12.

26. Virtually the same authority is accorded to eastern Patriarchs and Major Archbishops. Enchiridion 1999, Norm 9 (expanding earlier grants authority to include their giving the apostolic blessing); Enchiridion 1986, Norm 12. That those few prelates known as "patriarchs" in the West (e.g., the Patriarch of Lisbon) are not included hereunder is clear from the tenor of the grant and from 1983 CIC 438. Moreover, by a very recent grant (June 29, 2002), bishops may impart on what amounts to a fourth day of the year, the apostolic blessing and plenary indulgence, under the usual conditions, within a co-cathedral church that once been a cathedral but now, by legitimate authority, is no longer a diocesan cathedral. See the 2004 edition of the Enchiridion 1999, pp. 90–92. The hope may be expressed without disrespect that such highly specialized indulgences, applicable to such a *very* small number of situations, will not be needlessly multiplied to the detriment of the pastorally beneficial simplifications achieved in this area by the reforms of Pope Paul VI.

27. Enchiridion 1999, Norm 8; Enchiridion 1986, Norm 11.

28. Enchiridion 1999, Norm 10; Enchiridion 1986, Norm 13.

29. Enchiridion 1999, Norm 12; Enchiridion 1986, Norm 15.

local authority) nor to indulgences granted by cardinals (because such indulgences are offered only to those present). This rule obviously allows the Holy See to monitor local indulgence practices and to address problems that might arise before they spread too widely.

Norms for Indulgences Involving a Church Visitation

Christianity is not a purely intellectual or "spiritualized" religion. It takes seriously, and makes use of, physical objects in promoting the faith. A prime example of this is a church, a tangible, visible place where Christians gather to offer corporate worship to God. The very use of a church signifies unity and belonging.[30] Several indulgences include among their requirements a visitation to a church or oratory.[31] These visits must be made in accord with certain norms, however, lest they become little more than tourist excursions or, worse, spiritually hollow exercises with which "magical" properties eventually come to be associated.

The main requirement in regard to visiting a church or oratory is that the visitation be a devout one.[32] The offering of prayers at the site itself represents this devotion.[33] The minimum prayers that are

---

30. Among the many examples of this point that suggest themselves here, the canonical requirement that Baptism, the rite that confers membership in the Church, must usually take place in a church or oratory (see 1983 CIC 857 § 1 and 860 § 1) is typical.

31. See, e.g., Enchiridion 1999, conc. 21 (Saints and Blesseds), 31 (Diocesan Synod), and of course 33 (Holy Places). Other indulgences that would normally be carried out, under any but the most unusual circumstances, in a church or oratory, include all or parts of nos. 5, 7, 8, 11, 13, 16, and 26–28. A visitation to a church or oratory, animated by prayers, was, in earlier times, a very common requirement for the acquisition of most plenary indulgences. See Hagedorn, pp. 128–130 and de Angelis, nos. 82–84. It no longer is commonly required for plenary indulgences. *Favores ampliari*, it would seem that legitimately established shrines (1983 CIC 1230–1234) should qualify for purposes of indulgences, even if the shrine in question is not also a church.

32. Hagedorn, p. 128.

33. Occasionally, factors such as great crowds or repair work might seriously delay or even prevent some individuals from entering the public areas of the church or oratory. In such cases, *favores ampliari*, one's presence on the property, or even in the crowd gathered at the holy place, suffices for the physical visitation. See also Hagedorn, p. 129.

In very unusual cases, a church or oratory to which an indulgence might be attached could itself be destroyed but rebuilt on or near the same site and under the same title within 50 years. In such cases, indulgences attached to the original church or oratory revive with the reconstruction and rededication. Enchiridion 1999, Norm 16 § 1; Enchiridion 1986, Norm 19, 1°. It is, however, almost inconceivable how such a situation could arise and, under the new laws on indulgences, not already be adequately covered by the regular norms for visits to churches or oratories. Perhaps the norm is but a left-over from times when many special indulgences

prescribed are an *Our Father* and a *Creed*.[34] These prayers, because they specifically underscore the devotion *of the visitor* to the church or oratory, may not be counted toward other prayers that might be required for the indulgence being sought.[35] Circumstances permitting, of course, one would want to spend more time in prayer than is required for these two orations, and if possible, make a visit to the Blessed Sacrament, for this practice itself is an action enriched by an indulgence.[36]

When visits to a church or oratory are required to be made on certain day,[37] such visits can be made at any time from noon of the preceding day until midnight (11:59 PM) of day itself, thus giving one actually 36 hours in which to make the required visit.[38]

THE PRAYERS AND WORKS REQUIRED FOR INDULGENCES

Indulgences are not given for works or prayers that one is already obligated by law to perform.[39] Thus, attending Mass on Sunday, as one is required to do by canon law (CCC 1389 and 2042; 1983 CIC

---

were attached to specific holy sites. If this is true, it might be clearer if this norm were omitted in future editions of the Enchiridion.

34. Enchiridion 1999, Norm 19; Enchiridion 1986, Norm 22.

35. For example, prayers for the pope's intentions are required for plenary indulgences and the faithful may satisfy this requirement by an *Our Father* and a *Hail Mary*. Enchiridion 1999, Norm 20 § 5; Enchiridion 1986, Norm 23 § 5. These prayers, in particular the *Our Father*, might appear to overlap. Serving different ends, however, they demand separate recitation. Four indulgences, however, that call for a visit to a church or oratory seem to replicate the requirement applicable to all plenary indulgences of praying an *Our Father* and a *Creed*, namely, nos. 21 § 2 (Prayers to Saints and Blessed); 29 § 1, 2° (Prayers for the dead on All Saints Day); 31 (Diocesan Synod); and 33 § 1 (Visits to various sacred places). These should probably be seen as restatements of the obligation originally set out in Enchiridion 1999, Norm 19, and not obligations to be satisfied in addition to those earlier ones. It might be clearer if these reiterations were omitted in future editions of the Enchiridion.

36. See Enchiridion 1999, conc. 7. The Blessed Sacrament is to be reserved in all churches and ought to be reserved in most oratories. See 1983 CIC 934.

37. See, e.g., Enchiridion 1999, conc. 33 or the recent indulgence for Divine Mercy Sunday, discussed elsewhere.

38. Enchiridion 1999, Norm 14; Enchiridion 1986, Norm 17.

39. Enchiridion 1999, Norm 21 § 1; Enchiridion 1986, Norm 24. Note that indulgences are not offered for works or prayers commanded by "precept" (basically, a personal order from a competent superior, per 1983 CIC 49), but as this is a relatively rare situation in ecclesiastical life, it is not discussed here.

1247) would not satisfy the requirement laid down in various indulgences, say, to visit a church or oratory.[40] A religious who is bound by canon law (1983 CIC 663 § 3) to pray the Divine Office (Liturgy of the Hours) would not obtain the indulgence attached to, say, the *Magnificat* each evening at Vespers.[41] The notion of "required by law" should also extend to civil law, for example, if one were sentenced by a court to community service, one could not apply those efforts toward, say, a partial indulgence for service to the needy.[42] Or again, while one might well offer up the tediousness of being stuck in traffic for an indulgence,[43] one could not offer up the tediousness of, say, observing the speed limit when no one is looking.

On the other hand, the mere fact that someone is required to do something does not necessarily mean that he or she is required to do it *by law*. Unless the obligation is a *legal* one, the efforts one undertakes in the performance of other responsibilities can be indulgenced in any number of ways.[44] Indeed, helping Christians to understand how God's mercy flows through their daily actions, including those required by the drudgery of worldly duties, is one of chief themes animating the post-conciliar reform of indulgences in the first place. Performing one's duties is already a good thing; performing them with conscious advertence to one's desire for deeper communion with God and his Church and to one's desire to benefit as deeply as possible by that communion is even better.

---

40. If, however, one were to arrive notably early for Mass, or stay significantly beyond its completion, such that the "visit" to a church or oratory accomplished thereby was clearly distinct from performance of the canonical Mass obligation, one could apply such a visit, even though occasioned by the Mass obligation, toward an indulgence.

41. See Enchiridion 1999, conc. 17 § 2, 1°. Similarly, the indulgence offered would not be available to clergy who are already required to recite the Divine Office (see 1983 CIC 276 § 2, 3°). See also Apostolic Penitentiary, *Urbis et Orbis Decretum* (December 25, 2004) wherein, *inter alia*, clergy and religious who are bound by [canon] law to pray the Liturgy of Hours are offered a plenary indulgence, under the usual conditions, for offering *Vespers* and *Compline*, *before the Blessed Sacrament* (emphasis added), and by implication, not otherwise. *L'Osservatore Romano*, English Weekly edition, January 19, 2005.

42. See Enchiridion 1999, General Grant, conc. 2.

43. See Enchiridion 1999, General Grant, conc. 1.

44. See, e.g., Enchiridion 1999, General Grant, conc. 1, and the discussion of teachers doing their job in light of Enchiridion 1999, conc. 6.

Moreover, an explicit exception is made in the area of sacramental Confession, in that those who receive a penance that is also itself an indulgenced prayer or work, can by the performance of that action satisfy *both* the demands of their penance and acquire the indulgence attached to the prayer or work.[45] For example, if one were, as a penance, enjoined to pray a *Salve Regina*, the offering of that prayer, even though it were imposed as a penance, would also suffice for the acquisition of the indulgence attached to the *Salve Regina*.[46]

Finally, a few indulgences are offered for specific prayers or works that might in turn be part of larger patterns of prayer and works also indulgenced. An example here would be the indulgence offered for praying the *Salve Regina* (*Hail Holy Queen*) and that offered for praying the Rosary, of which the *Salve Regina* is commonly a part.[47] Or again, some indulgenced prayers and actions can clearly be performed in the course of pursuing other indulgences, such praying a Rosary while making an indulgenced visit to a church or oratory.[48] Without becoming grasping or calculating in the matter, the rule seems to be this: prayers and works, even if indulgenced separately, which are a necessary part of another indulgence one is seeking (as, for example, the *Magnificat* is a necessary part of Evening Prayer for the Dead) would not suffice for a second, presumably smaller indulgence within the larger. On the other hand, where the performance of one indulgence simply provides a suitable occasion for acquiring another independently of the first (as an indulgenced visit to a church or oratory might provide the occasion for saying a Rosary), then separate indulgences could be acquired.[49]

---

45. See Enchiridion 1999, Norm 21 § 2; Enchiridion 1986, Norm 24. Many, perhaps most, penances would seem to fall within the description of prayers and actions given in, say, Enchiridion 1999, conc. 15 (mental prayer) or the first three General Grants.

46. See Enchiridion 1999, conc. 17 § 2, 3°.

47. See Enchiridion 1999, conc. 17 § 2, 3°, and 17 § 1, 1°, respectively.

48. See Enchiridion 1999, conc. 17 § 1, 1°, and, e.g. Enchiridion 1999, conc. 33, respectively.

49. Note that nothing prevents one seeking an indulgence for, say, a visit to a church, from using the Rosary not as a vehicle for acquiring a second indulgence, but rather as means to augmenting one's disposition toward acquiring the first. It is certainly a choice that can be left to the individual who might wish simply to hand the matter over to God and let him show his generosity as he sees is best for the individual.

Not all indulgences require specific prayers to be said,[50] and of these, only some insist that a given text of a prayer to be used.[51] There is, I suggest a positive and negative reason for this. Positively, such an approach protects the freedom of the faithful to form private prayers in accord with their own situations and inclinations. It respects a right of self-direction that, while inappropriate in, say, a liturgical setting,[52] is quite becoming in an area that draws on personal devotional motives. Negatively, if we may put it that way, the lack of insistence on the need for using certain prayers and especially on certain texts of prayers might reflect the practical difficulties, perhaps even the impossibility, of arriving at universally acceptable texts in such areas. Even a passing familiarity with textual variants in prayers, including such a fundamental one as the *Our Father*, shows how many doctrinally sound versions of prayers there are (to say nothing of those of creeping heterodoxy). Because no specific language is demanded in the use of any prayers to which indulgences are attached, any translation or version approved by competent authority (and admittedly, those are many) suffice for use in indulgences.[53]

As for the manner in which prayers should be offered, there is great flexibility shown here as well. Some indulgences, of course,

---

50. This point, perhaps because it is so frequently asserted, is easy to overlook. For example, Enchiridion 1999, conc. 19, provides indulgences for prayers (*Preces*, in the plural) in honor of Saint Joseph and authorizes the use of a "legitimately approved prayer" without identifying which prayers those are, and lists only by way of example (using the illustrative "*e.g.*") the "*Ad te, beate Iospeh*". The 1950 Enchiridion nos. 458–479 listed, in contrast, at least a dozen indulgenced prayers to Saint Joseph (one of which was the *Ad te, beate Ioseph*), not counting hymns, litanies, pious exercises, and little offices in his honor. But see Enchiridion 1999, conc. 20, authorizing only one prayer to Saints Peter and Paul, despite being titled *Preces in honorem Ss. Apostolorum Petri et Pauli*. This should be clarified in future editions of the Enchiridion. Indulgences that call only for a "legitimately approved prayer" to be used are: conc. 1; 7 § 2, 2°; 8 § 2, 2°; 9, 2°; 11 § 2; 14 § 1; 15 (any mental prayer); 17 § 2, 3°; 18; 19; 21 § 1; 22; 24; 25, 1°; 26 § 2; 28 § 1; 28 § 2, 1°; 28 § 2, 4°; 29 § 1, 1°; and 29 § 2, 1°.

51. Those indulgences that do require specific prayers to be said are: Enchiridion 1999, conc. 2; 3; 7 § 1, 2°; 8 § 1, 2°; 14 § 1 (requiring a Profession of Faith, but not specifying a formula); 17 § 1, 1° (requiring a Rosary, but leaving options as to its length); 17 § 2, 1°; 17 § 2, 2°; 20; 21 § 2 (questionably, since it appears to reiterate a prayer requirement already arising from Norm 19); 23; 25, 2°; 26 § 1; 28 § 2, 2°; 28 § 2, 3° (offering two options for a Profession of Faith); 29 § 1, 2°; 29 § 2, 2° (offering options from the Liturgy of the Hours and the *Requiem*); 31; and 33 § 1.

52. 1983 CIC 837, 846.

53. Enchiridion 1999, Norms 22; Enchiridion 1986, Norm 25.

require no prayer at all[54] (however appropriate it might be to begin or
end such undertakings with prayer) while others require no more than
"mental prayer" otherwise unspecified as to content.[55] The typical
model of offering prayer is, of course, oral recitation, alone or with a
group.[56] Alternation of words between persons is, however, expressly
approved, as is the practice of simply mentally following the prayers
that another leads.[57] Particular postures in prayer are not required.[58]
Older questions about the sufficiency of an individual reciting prescribed prayers *only* mentally (see, e.g., 1917 CIC 934 § 1, which was
not carried into the 1983 Code) are not treated in the current norms,
but I suggest that such questions now pertain more to the disposition
of the actor. Those who can devoutly offer these prayers mentally
should feel free to do so; those who desire the extra discipline of oral
recitation in private prayer should use it.

WHAT ARE "PIOUS INVOCATIONS"?

Pious invocations are very short expressions or thoughts that help raise
the mind to God.[59] Pious invocations are to be seen not as additional
acts alongside various indulgences, but rather as being woven into
the prayers and works of the indulgences themselves.[60] They may be
expressed orally or mentally. Although many suggestions for pious

---

54. Enchiridion 1999, nos. 6; 9, 1°; 12 (requiring no prayers by the recipient of the indulgence); 16 § 1; and 30.

55. See, e.g., Enchiridion 1999, no. 15. One might also include here requirements devoutly
or piously "to assist" at certain events, without expressly calling for prayer, such as conc. 5
(religious purposes); 27 § 1, 2° (first Mass); 27 § 2, 3° (ordination anniversary); 29 § 1, 1° (for
the dead).

56. The term "publicly" is not always used consistently in Church documents. For instance,
when an indulgence calls for prayers to be offered "publicly" (e.g., Enchiridion 1999, conc. 2
or 3), it probably means "in the presence of at least one other person" (who need not join in the
prayer). The tenor of these grants does not require that the recitation of the prayer take place
in a liturgical setting, or even in a church or oratory (*pace*, Raccolta, Preface no. 7), in order to
satisfy the requirements for the plenary indulgence.

57. See Enchiridion 1999, Norms 23; Enchiridion 1986, Norm 26. See also Enchiridion
1999, Norm 26 (also Enchiridion 1986, Norm 29) making provision for the deaf and mute to
sign their prayers or simply to follow prayers mentally for the acquisition of indulgences.

58. De Angelis, no. 94; Hagedorn, p. 114.

59. Enchiridion 1999, Pious Invocations, §1, 3; Enchiridion 1986, Pious Invocations, §§ 1, 3.

60. Unlike the case under pre-conciliar legislation on indulgences, pious invocations themselves are no longer explicitly indulgenced, although, strictly speaking, they would appear to
be sufficient, standing alone, as mental prayers under Enchiridion 1999, no. 15 (Mental prayer).

invocations are offered, any such formulas, even those spontaneously conceived by the faithful, suffice for use in indulgences. What is more important than specific terminology is that the invocation be accommodated to the needs and circumstances of the faithful and to the exigencies of the moment or indulgence at hand.[61]

Examples of pious invocations abound[62] but some seem especially noteworthy, including: "My God"; "Jesus"; "Praise be Jesus Christ"; "Jesus, Mary, and Joseph"; "Blessed be God"; "Your will be done"; "God help me"; "Lord be merciful to me a sinner"; "My Lord and my God"; "Jesus, Mary, and Joseph"; and "Father, into your hands I commend my spirit." One cannot help but to notice how some of these invocations have also been hijacked into occasions for taking the name of the Lord in vain, and in that sense, they would seem especially worthy for use by Christians desirous of making reparations for their sins and the sins of the world.[63]

This completes our look at some of the questions people have regarding the operation of indulgences that go beyond what we can learn by looking at the definition of an indulgences, and we are now ready to turn our attention to the actual indulgences that are currently in force in the Catholic Church. As we will see, the indulgences now in force can be organized and fruitfully studied in different ways, though no one way especially better than another. However, even that point will be more clear once we begin to look at the specific indulgences now in effect.

---

61. Enchiridion 1999, Pious Invocations, § 2; Enchiridion 1986, Pious Invocations, §2.

62. There are, for example, scores of invocations throughout the Raccolta.

63. Reparation for various blasphemies was, in fact, recommended in the Raccolta, nos. 8, 241, 328–329, 367, and 696.

Chapter 5

Current Grants of Indulgences

It is time to study carefully the two modern types of indulgences, then the actual indulgences that are currently available within each type. In essentials, of course, all indulgences are alike,[1] but for purposes of organizing, explaining, and incorporating them into one's life as a Christian, various categories are useful. Besides the very common distinction among indulgences whether they are plenary and partial, a second important way of categorizing indulgences now exists, namely, that of dividing indulgences into what we may call "General Grant Indulgences" and "Specific Grant Indulgences."

GENERAL GRANT INDULGENCES

Central to the post-conciliar reform of indulgences by Pope Paul VI was the idea that indulgences—and the spirit of contrition, penance, charity, and desire for reconciliation with God that they foster— should no longer be seen as acts unconnected to normal Christian life, but rather should be incorporated into the daily life of Catholics. To accomplish this goal, the Holy Father organized a completely new category of indulgences known as "General Grant Indulgences." It is easy to overlook these indulgences because, unlike those of past centuries, they do not seem to be oriented to specific tasks. It is, in that sense, a little harder to tell when one has "done" them. And yet these indulgences are listed first in the Enchiridion precisely because they are intended to be the faithful's primary participation in these special gifts of God through his Church. Moreover, to Pope Paul VI's

---

1. Hagedorn, p. 64.

original three General Grant Indulgences, a fourth was added by Pope John Paul II in the Enchiridion 1999.[2] They are as follows.

> 5.1.1. The first general grant of a partial indulgence applies to those who, in the course of performing their daily duties or in patiently bearing with the difficulties of life, humbly raise their thoughts to God and offer Him a pious invocation.[3]

This first indulgence rests on, among others things, the words of Christ to pray without ceasing (Luke 18:1; see also 1 Thessalonians 5:17). It is designed to help the Christian make part of the very fabric of daily life a constant awareness of the presence and love of God.[4] There simply is no end to the examples that come to mind by which this indulgence can be obtained: a child doing homework, a mother doing laundry, or, venturing a personal favorite here, a father accepting a traffic jam on his way home from work, if done by one who invokes the help of God therein, all of these may obtain this indulgence. Bearing the consequences of injustice, or even just the thoughtlessness of others, is even harder, but such acts are even more pleasing to God who sees all and who bore with incalculably worse at our hands.

Acts calling for exercises in patience on our part seem especially pleasing to God, for our impatience to get about performing our duties or pursuing good ends often masks a dangerous pride which pretends that everything depends on us and our efforts, instead of on God and his providence. Asking God for the grace of patience is a very good way to thank him for showing patience with us while we slowly come to a deeper appreciation of how much we have offended him by sin, and how much he loves us by patiently awaiting our ever deeper return to him.

---

2. As was noted in the Introduction to this work, the first three versions of the post-conciliar Enchiridion (June 1968, October 1968, and 1986) are very similar in organization, and specifically, indulgences themselves are presented in alphabetical order in Latin. The version released in 1999, however, is not only augmented in places, but organizationally is very different from the earlier three editions, with indulgences now being grouped around spiritual themes. To make the present study as useful and as practicable with all of these versions, wherever possible, citations to the current Enchiridion 1999 will be followed by citations to the Enchiridion 1986 so that the development of the current norms and grants may be the more easily studied.

3. Enchiridion 1999, General Grant, conc. 1; Enchiridion 1986, General Grant, conc. 1. See also Raccolta, no. 766 (although the terminology used there suggests that we should limit the indulgence to those who raise the mind to God during work or labor only.)

4. Enchiridion 1999, Introduction, no. 4. See also Pope John XXIII's grant of an indulgence to those who offer their day's work to God, in *Canon Law Digest* V: 448.

One can readily see that forming the intention to gain indulgences under the first General Grant all but demands the establishment of a habitual intention to gain indulgences, for there are obviously too many instances in the day to recall the appropriateness of offering something up each time.[5] And yet, striving to see God's place in every event of life is also quite good. As suggested earlier, a compromise might be this: Besides forming and renewing the habitual intention to obtain indulgences say, once a year, one should make this same desire a part of one's morning prayers. Then, when events arise in the course of the day requiring extra efforts on our part, we should call to mind our love for God, expressed in a pious invocation, and go on about life. Even this small exercise will become "second nature" over time.

> 5.1.2. The second general grant of a partial indulgence applies to those who, led by a spirit of Faith, give of themselves or their goods in compassionate service to those in need.[6]

This indulgence encourages the Christian faithful to be especially mindful of the needs of others, and to strive to meet those needs in accord with the resources and opportunities that God has given us. This indulgence does not reward every act of kindness; rather, it applies to those who undertake to make a gift of time or goods to those in need. The needy would include the poor, of course, but also those in need of instruction, those with emotional needs such as loneliness, and so on.

Since shortly after the Council of Trent, indulgences attached to alms-giving, at least those for which ecclesiastical authority was the beneficiary of the donations, have been forbidden.[7] While there is nothing intrinsically wrong with having monetary donations serve as the material expression of charity, and while such gifts can under certain circumstances do great good, the temptation to see indulgences as something to be purchased was too great, at least for fallen human

---

5. See Preliminary Comments to the Four General Grants, § 2, wherein, speaking directly of General Grant, conc. 1, we read "These kinds of acts [i.e., forming the intention to gain indulgences for such small undertakings], owing to human frailty, are not frequent."

6. Enchiridion 1999, General Grant, conc. 2; Enchiridion 1986, General Grant, conc. 2.

7. See Pope Saint Pius V, con. *Etsi Dominici gregis*, 8 February 1567, appearing as Doc. 118, in P. Gasparri, ed., *Fontes Codicis Iuris Canonici*, in 9 vols., vol. I: 209–211, capping a series of ever tightening papal restrictions on indulgences for money.

beings. That said, there is no express provision against individuals offering alms to other persons or organizations besides ecclesiastical ones, and having that gift of self, as represented by money, serve as one's sign of service. One must, however, even here be on guard lest money become a convenient substitute for a genuine gift of self. Moreover, generosity is not measured by the amount of the gift, but by the resources of the giver.[8]

> 5.1.3. The third general grant of a partial indulgence applies to those who, in a spirit of penitence, freely abstain from something that is otherwise licit for them.[9]

It is no secret that many Christians today have lost the sense of penance in their lives (CCC 2043; 1983 CIC 1249). No doubt many factors have contributed to this, but what is needed now is a renewal of appreciation for how penance is really a part of a healthy life in faith.

This indulgence enjoys a long history of observance by the faithful, the "offering up" of something that itself is a good. It can be as subtle as not taking sugar in one's tea or foregoing one's favorite television show, or it can extend even to the great acts of mortification undertaken in the lives of the saints. It is always advisable, though, before undertaking more strenuous penances to seek sound advice from one's spiritual director, lest pride in one's penances infiltrate one's motives or harm to self or others (say, by way of setting a confusing example) arise unknowingly.

As is generally true of all indulgences, this one is not obtained by those who are already required by law to perform a penitential act, such as abstaining from meat on Fridays in Lent (1983 CIC 1250–1253), with the one exception we have already seen: if a penance is imposed in sacramental Confession, that same act can be the subject of an indulgence.[10]

---

8. Recall the story of the widow's mite in Mark 21 and Luke 21.

9. Enchiridion 1999, General Grant, conc. 3; Enchiridion 1986, General Grant, conc. 3.

10. Enchiridion 1999, Norm 21 § 2; Enchiridion 1986, Norm 24. There seems no longer a reason why, indeed, almost every penance imposed in sacramental Confession could not be made the object of the partial indulgences attached to, say, the specific prayers that might be assigned, to mental prayer, the reading of Sacred Scripture, even to acts of charity. Given the close association between Confession and the historical growth of indulgences, there seems to be a genuine appropriateness in making the performance of one's penances the occasion of

5.1.4. The fourth general grant of a partial indulgence applies to those who, in open witness to faith, render a sign of their belief before others.[11]

This grant is new with the Enchiridion 1999. As with all General Grant Indulgences, the list of potential examples here is enormous. Such a witness to faith could be as small as saying grace before meals in a restaurant, or weightier acts such as standing in prayerful protest against an abortion clinic with other members of one's parish or diocese. The point is that Christians are called to proclaim the Gospel throughout their daily lives (1983 CIC 225 § 2). In an age where religious belief is at best relegated to private life (and at worst, scorned), the making of an appropriate gesture of faith before strangers is not as easy as it seems. Is there a risk that some will perform inappropriate or ostentatious acts in a misguided attempt to win this indulgence or inflate its value? Perhaps, and such cases would call for gentle but firm correction. The greater risk, though, one already with us, is that believing Christians, content to let their faith show on Sundays or within the home, never dream of carrying their witness to the world that so desperately needs it. This indulgence encourages the faithful to consider precisely that kind of action.

SPECIFIC GRANT INDULGENCES

For many centuries, all indulgences in the Church were what we today would call "Specific Grant Indulgences," for indulgences used to be tied to reciting specific prayers or undertaking specific actions.[12] Today, though, in keeping with Pope Paul VI's goals as discussed in

---

an indulgence as well. Against this opinion, though, there stand various learned opinions, e.g., Hagedorn pp. 102–103 and the traditional language of Enchiridion 1999, Norm 24, which seems to restrict the possibility of serving double purposes to performing penances that are also indulgenced prayers or works. Such a narrow reading seemed more supportable when, prior to the reforms of Paul VI, indulgences were indeed specifically delineated prayers and works. With the advent of General Grant Indulgences, however, and the emphasis on weaving the practice of indulgences into the very fabric of the Christian life, such a sharp demarcation between "penances" and "indulgenced prayers and works" seems less supportable. Indeed, the fact that such special penances are undertaken immediately after sacramental Confession and in a spirit of gratitude to God for his great mercy and humble acceptance of the authority of his ministers would seem to augment the disposition of the faithful who seek indulgences at those grace-filled times.

11. Enchiridion 1999, General Grant, conc. 4.

12. The norms and grants of the 1957 Raccolta, for example, runs to over 600 pages and is overwhelmingly geared to offering specific prayers and performing specific actions.

our treatment of General Grant Indulgences, Specific Grant Indulgences, while they have been retained as a category, have been greatly reduced in number.[13] In deciding which Specific Grant Indulgences to retain, the pope gave special attention to those prayers and actions that could claim a long tradition in the Church or that had attracted a widespread popularity among the faithful. This will become apparent when we look at Specific Grant Indulgences in more detail. One of the chief advantages of Specific Grant Indulgences, of course, is that they provide sound examples of worthy prayers and actions and are of help to those who might not, for whatever reason, be accustomed to developing such practices on their own. By using them, one also can be sure that the wisdom of the Church is behind the texts given or the action described, and *that* is a real help against sincere but mistaken spiritualities or other idiosyncrasies creeping into one's faith life.

Most Specific Grant Indulgences are partial, but under certain conditions, they can be augmented to plenary. Specific Grant Indulgences consist of prayers and actions with prayers,[14] which in turn may be categorized in several different ways. For purposes of this presentation,[15] Special Grant Indulgences have been divided into four broad types:

1. Individual, usually shorter, prayers that can be said under almost any circumstances;
2. Longer prayers or those that should or may be offered under certain circumstances;
3. Specific, substantial actions or activities that may be undertaken at the faithful's initiative;

---

13. The norms and grants of the 1986 Enchiridion run just 70 pages, with only about 60 of those pages being devoted to Specific Grant Indulgences.

14. For some Specific Grant Indulgences, it is not terribly clear whether one is dealing with a prayer with an action, or an action with a prayer. The distinction is academically interesting, but not crucial to one's efforts in obtaining the indulgence in practice.

15. As noted earlier, the Holy See has varied in its own method of cataloguing indulgences since Paul VI's reforms. For example, up though the 1986 Enchiridion, Specific Grant Indulgences were listed alphabetically by prayer or description of action, whereas the 1999 Enchiridion organizes indulgences by spiritual theme. No system is entirely satisfactory, since indulgences span such a wide variety of human and spiritual activity. The system adopted here basically presents four types of Specific Grant indulgences by the ease of their acquisition, beginning with those requiring the lightest effort, moving to those demanding somewhat more planning, and finally ending with those that are offered only on certain occasions, such that the faithful need to anticipate and prepare for them in order to obtain them.

4. Special occasions or events in which the faithful are invited to take advantage.

Individual Short Prayers—Almost Any Circumstance

A variety of short prayers are the subject of indulgences today. Unless indicated otherwise, all of these indulgences are partial, to be obtained under the usual rules for all partial indulgences.[16] While earlier collections of indulgences listed many such prayers, far fewer prayers are indulgenced today, their number limited to those with a special history of devotional use by Christians over time.[17] The indulgences discussed here follow the order in which they are presented in the Enchiridion, although a discussion of the use of objects of devotion, being applicable to many specific indulgences, opens this section.

General Use of Objects of Devotion in Prayer.[18] A partial indulgence is offered to the faithful whenever, in lifting their hearts and minds to God in prayer,[19] they make use of an object of devotion blessed by any cleric, from deacon to pope. To suffice for this indulgence, the object must be one of devotion (such as a cross or crucifix, a rosary, a scapular, a holy image or statute, etc.) and not simply be an object that was blessed, such as a house, an automobile, etc., however praiseworthy such blessings are. Moreover, any blessing by a cleric suffices, though more formal blessings often contribute to the disposition of those making use of such objects.[20] One should, of course, be on guard

---

16. Enchiridion 1999, Norm 17; Enchiridion 1986, Norm 20.

17. The very fact that most such prayers have been used by Christians over a long period of time implies that translations of those prayers also have varied over time. While each prayer typically has a single official (usually in Latin) formula, it usually has several acceptable translations. One has but to compare the English translations of several indulgenced prayers as set forth in 1968 Enchiridion with the English translation of exactly the same prayers set forth in 1986 Enchiridion to see how widely even approved translations can vary. In any event, good translations of prayers are available in a wide variety of formats.

18. *Obiectorum pietatis usus.* Enchiridion 1999, conc. 14 § 2; Enchiridion 1986, conc. 35. See also Enchiridion 1999, Norm 15; Enchiridion 1986, conc. 18.

19. Obviously, such prayers might themselves be indulgenced, in which case the indulgence obtained is enhanced by the use of the blessed object, for its use in prayer contributes to the disposition of the individual.

20. A simple sign of the cross, with or even without the Trinitarian formula, suffices for a blessing. For more formal blessings, see generally, *Book of Blessings*, Part IV: Blessing of articles meant to foster the devotion of the Christian people, and *Shorter Book of Blessings,* Part III: Blessing of articles meant to foster the devotion of the Christian people. If the object was

against thinking that the object being devoutly used has acquired a special power in virtue of the blessing or indulgence or that some sort of magic is at work in them. The focus of blessings, as of indulgences, is the individual who makes proper use of them to move closer to God. Also, as a guard against "trafficking in indulgences" (1917 CIC 2327), any indulgences attached to an object of devotion cease when the object is sold (for *any* price)—but not when it is freely lent or given away— and when the object is destroyed.[21]

We can now begin our examination of the shorter prayers currently listed in the Enchiridion 1999.

Prayer for Christian Unity.[22] Unity among Christians is a Gospel imperative (John 17: 20–21; CCC 813–822; 1983 CIC 383 § 3, 755 § 1). The Christian faithful who offer any approved prayers for that intention may obtain a partial indulgence thereby. A suggested prayer is *Omnipotens et misericors Deus* (*All powerful and merciful God*). A plenary indulgence for participation in certain activities designed to promote Christian unity is discussed later.

Mental Prayer.[23] The sense of "mental prayer" envisioned here goes beyond simply praying without audible words. It probably also transcends the use of traditional or formulaic prayers, especially those already indulgenced elsewhere, although such standardized prayers might be a good way to get started in mental prayer.[24] Instead, what this indulgence seeks to encourage is extemporaneous, personal prayer arising from the circumstances of one's own life. No minimum amount of time in prayer is specified for the acquisition of the indulgence, and the prayer may be of any character, that is, it may be prayer of supplication, thanksgiving, adoration, and so on. It does seem, though, that the man-

blessed by the pope or by a bishop, it might be used for a plenary indulgence under certain conditions, discussed elsewhere.

21. Enchiridion 1999, Norm 16 § 2; Enchiridion 1986, Norm 19 § 2. An indulgenced object that is stolen, as well as one that is damaged beyond reasonable repair, would also seem to lose the indulgence.

22. *Hebdomada pro christianorum unitate.* Enchiridion 1999, conc. 11 § 2; Enchiridion 1986, conc. 44. See also Raccolta, no. 622.

23. *Oratio mentalis.* Enchiridion 1999, conc. 15; Enchiridion 1986, conc. 38. See also Raccolta, no. 688 (establishing 15 minutes as the minimum time in prayer required for the indulgence).

24. In this respect the Raccolta would provide much by way of example.

ner of the prayer precisely as *mental* (as opposed to, say, spontaneous prayer, which could be mental or vocal) is the express point of the indulgence, and thus the equivalent prayer offered orally, while valuable in its own right of course, does not seem to be indulgenced hereby.

Shorter Prayers to the Most Blessed Virgin Mary.[25] Several shorter prayers to Our Lady are augmented with partial indulgences.[26] Those prayers are: the *Magnificat*,[27] the *Angelus* or *Regina Coeli*,[28] the *Maria, Mater gratiae* (*A Child's Prayer to Mary*), the *Memorare* (*Remember O most gracious Virgin Mary*),[29] the *Salve Regina* (*Hail Holy Queen*),[30] the *Santa Maria succurre nobis* (*Mary Help of Those in Need*),[31] and the *Sub tuum praesidium* (*Ancient Prayer to Our Lady*).[32]

Angel of God.[33] A partial indulgence is available to those who invoke the aid of their guardian angel (CCC 334–336), by any approved prayer.

---

25. *Preces ad Beatissimam Virginem Mariam.* Enchiridion 1999, conc. 17 § 2; Enchiridion 1986, conc. 9 (*Angelus* and *Regina Coeli*), 30 (*Magnificat*), 31 (*Maria, Mater gratiae*), 32 (*Memorare*), 51 (*Salve Regina*), 52 (*Santa Maria succurre nobis*), and 57 (*Sub tuum praesidium*).

26. As is usually true of indulgences attached to specific prayers in honor of the saints and angels, the list offered here is only illustrative, and other approved prayers to Our Lady would satisfy for this indulgence. Purely spontaneous prayers to Mary may be indulgenced under, for example, Enchiridion 1999, General Grant, conc. 1 or Specific Grants, conc. 15. See also Specific Grant, conc. 21.

27. Among shorter Marian prayers, the great *Magnificat* has a certain pride of place, it having been prayed by Mary herself, as recorded in Scripture (Luke 1: 46–55). It is used in every Vespers (Evening Prayer) of the Liturgy of the Hours. See also Raccolta, no. 320.

28. These prayers may be recited at any hour of the day, but traditionally they are offered at dawn, midday, and sunset. A fixed time (such as 6 AM, Noon, and 6 PM) is not required, but is often observed. The preference sometimes expressed that the prayers be recited slightly after the hour is not carried into the current discipline. While the "Angelus" is the more common prayer, the "Regina Caeli" is said (or more often, sung) in its place during Easter season (which begins on Easter Sunday and runs up to Pentecost). See also Raccolta, no. 331.

29. See also Raccolta, no. 339.

30. This great prayer often concludes, of course, the Rosary, but its splendor also recommends it as a "stand-alone" prayer to Our Lady. As noted elsewhere, when prayed as part of the Rosary, the *Salve Regina* is not separately indulgenced. See also Raccolta, no. 332.

31. See also Raccolta, no. 349.

32. See also Raccolta, no. 333.

33. *Preces ad custodem Angelum.* Enchiridion 1999, conc. 18; Enchiridion 1986, conc. 8. See also Raccolta, no. 452.

Invocation of Saint Peter and Paul.[34] A partial indulgence is available to those who invoke the intercession of Saint Peter and Paul. For this indulgence, the specific prayer *Sancti Apostoli Petre et Paule* (*Holy Apostles Peter and Paul*) must be used.

Prayer for Benefactors.[35] A partial indulgence is available to those who offer prayers for their benefactors, using any approved formula. This indulgence requires that one be moved by something more than natural gratitude, that one, in other words, recognize and give thanks for the divine element in the benefactions one has experienced at the hands of others. The spirit of this prayer must be more than just a reciprocal favor of, say, generally praying for a benefactor's intention or welfare. The indulgence attaches to prayers that are animated specifi-cally by gratitude and, in that sense, fosters humility in the one offer-ing such thanks. A common prayer for benefactors is *Retribuere dig-nare, Domine* (*Grant, O Lord, for Thy name's sake*).

Prayers for Pastors.[36] This partial indulgence enriches prayers for the pope offered anytime, and for diocesan or eparchial bishops offered at the outset of their pastoral duties or on their anniversaries. Although these prayers need not be offered within a liturgical celebration of those duties, that for diocesan and eparchial bishops may be found in the Missal, generally at the first oration (or Opening Prayer, or *Collect*) in the liturgy used at the bishop's installation or on their anniversary. The prayer suggested for the pope, on the other hand, is the well-known *Oremus pro Pontifice* (*Let us pray for the Pope*).

---

34. *Preces in honorem Ss. Apostolorum Petri et Pauli.* Enchiridion 1999, conc. 20; Enchiridion 1986, conc. 53. Raccolta no. 480. It would seem that in this case, the indulgence should have been titled *Prex in honorem . . .* (*Prayer* in honor . . .), because only one prayer option is offered. See also Enchiridion 1999, conc. 33 for an indulgence available on the Feast of Saints Peter and Paul.

35. *Preces pro benefactoribus.* Enchiridion 1999, conc. 24; Enchiridion 1986, conc. 47 (wherein the requirement of supernatural gratitude was not explicitly set out). See also Raccolta, no. 666.

36. *Preces pro pastoribus.* Enchiridion 1999, conc. 25; Enchiridion 1986, conc. 39 (wherein only prayer for the pope was indulgenced). See also Raccolta, no. 650 (for the pope); no. 672 (parish priests).

Shorter Prayers of Supplication or Thanksgiving.[37] Besides the two great prayers of supplication and thanksgiving that are enriched with a plenary indulgence,[38] many shorter prayers are the subject of partial indulgences, especially: *Actiones nostras* (Prayer for all Occasions);[39] *Adsumus* (Prayer before Meetings);[40] *Agimus tibi gratias* (A Prayer of Thanksgiving);[41] *Benedic, Domine nos* (Blessing before Meals); *Domine, Deus omnipotens* (Prayer at the Start of the Day);[42] *Exaudi nos* (Prayer for the Household); *Veni, Sancte Spiritus* (Come, Holy Spirit); *Visita, quaesumus, Domine* (Prayer at Night).[43]

Renewal of Baptismal promises.[44] A partial indulgence is offered to those faithful who renew their baptismal promises. Any approved formula satisfies here.

Prayers for the Dead.[45] Offering the prayer *Requiem aeternam* (Eternal rest) obtains a partial indulgence that is applicable only to the faithful departed.[46] As Pope Paul VI observed, "And if the faithful

---

37. *Preces supplicationis et gratiarum actionis.* Enchiridion 1999, conc. 26 § 2; Enchiridion 1986, conc. 1 (*Actiones nostras*); 5 (*Adsumus*); 7 (*Agimus tibi gratias*); 21 (*Domine, Deus omnipotens*); 24 (*Exaudi nos*); 62 (*Veni, Sancte Spiritus*); 64 (*Visita, quaesumus, Domine*). The prayer *Benedic, Domine nos*, was not expressly indulged before the Enchiridion 1999. Circumstances might also suggest the use at mealtimes at least of the "Blessing before or after Meals" contained in the *Book of Blessings*, Chap. 23; *Shorter Book of Blessings*, Chap. 5, which blessings would clearly satisfy the indulgence requirements. See also Raccolta, no. 282 (*Veni, Sancte Spiritus*).

38. Namely, the *Veni, Creator* and the *Te Deum*, referred to under Enchiridion 1999, Norm 26 § 1.

39. See also Raccolta, no. 680.

40. See also Raccolta, no. 682. Not yet a very common prayer in English-speaking lands, perhaps, but one that can be used before meetings not simply of a religious character (say, meetings of the parish council) but anytime Christians come together to purse a common goal. Circumstances might also suggest the use of the "Blessing of Those Gathered at a Meeting" contained in the *Book of Blessings*, Chap. 6; *Shorter Book of Blessings*, Chap. 5, which blessing would clearly satisfy the indulgence requirements.

41. See also Raccolta, no. 683.

42. Raccolta, no. 60.

43. Raccolta, no. 62.

44. *Professio Fidei et actus virtutum theologalium.* Enchiridion 1999, conc. 28 § 2, 1°; Enchiridion 1986, conc. 70. This same renewal of one's profession of faith is the subject of a plenary indulgence at certain times. See Enchiridion 1999, conc. 28 § 1.

45. *Pro fidelibus defunctis.* Enchiridion 1999, conc. 29 § 2, 2°; Enchiridion 1986, conc. 46. The Raccolta had many indulgenced prayers for the dead, beginning at no. 582. Note that all indulgences available under this grant may be applied *only* to the poor souls in Purgatory.

46. This grant (which presents the Office of the Dead as an optional prayer) seems a good case to recall that the worth of partial indulgences depends in part on the intrinsic merit of the

offer indulgences in suffrage for the dead, they cultivate charity in an excellent way and while raising their minds to heaven, they bring a wiser order into the things of this world."[47]

Longer Prayers—Offered under Certain Circumstances

Various longer prayers are the subject of indulgences today. Unless indicated otherwise, all of these indulgences are partial, to be obtained under the usual circumstances for partial indulgences.[48] While earlier collections of indulgences listed many such prayers, far fewer prayers are indulgenced today, their number limited to those that have a special history of devotional use by Christians over time.[49] The indulgences discussed here follow the order in which they are presented in the Enchiridion 1999. Earlier comments about the use of objects of devotion in pursuing these indulgences should be borne in mind.

Consecration of the human race to Christ the King.[50] Normally, the indulgence attached to this prayer *Iesu dulcissime, Redemptor (Most Sweet Jesus, Redeemer)*, which may be recited at any time, is partial, but if

---

prayer or action undertaken. Obviously, to offer Morning or Evening Prayer for the dead (Enchiridion 1999, conc. 29 § 2, 2°) is a more substantial undertaking than offering the simple prayer "Eternal rest" would be, and in that regard it would be of greater benefit to the poor souls. On the other hand, "Eternal rest" can be said for the faithful departed more frequently (if only because it is much shorter) than can prayers from the Liturgy of the Hours.

47. *Doctrina*, no. 8. See also CCC 958, 1032; 1983 CIC 994. As a reminder, any indulgence *may* be offered for the dead, but some indulgences, so designated, *must* be offered for the dead. It seems to be an open question as to whether indulgences can be applied to the dead who were not baptized, although clearly non-baptized persons cannot obtain indulgences in this life. Given the fact that all indulgences for the dead are applied by way of suffrage (discussed elsewhere), it seems permissible for one simply to go ahead and offer indulgences on behalf of those whom ones knows or reasonably believes not to have been baptized, and, as is the case with all such indulgences, trusting God to apply them as he sees fit.

48. Enchiridion 1999, Norm 17; Enchiridion 1986, Norm 20.

49. As noted elsewhere, the very fact that most such prayers have been used by Christians over a long period of time implies that translations of those prayers also have varied over time. While each prayer typically has a single official formula, it usually has several acceptable translations. One has but to compare the English translations of several indulged prayers as set forth in Enchiridion 1968 with the English translation of the exact same prayers set forth in Enchiridion 1986 to see how widely even approved translations can vary. In any event, good translations of prayers are available in a wide variety of formats.

50. *Actus dedicationis humani generis Iesu Christo Regi.* Enchiridion 1999, conc. 2; Enchiridion 1986, conc. 27. See also Raccolta, no. 271. Do not confuse this prayer, *Iesu dulcissime, Redemptor*, with the *Iesu dulcissim [cuius effusa]* which is used for the indulgence attached to the Act of Reparation in Enchiridion 1999, conc. 3.

the prayer is offered publicly on the Feast of Christ the King (the last Sunday in Ordinary time, that is, the Sunday before the First Sunday of Advent), the indulgence offered is plenary under the usual conditions.

An Act of Reparation to the Sacred Heart.[51] Devotion to the Sacred Heart of Jesus has been encouraged by popes for centuries. Two saints, Margaret Mary Alacoque (1647–1690) and Maria Faustina Kowalska (1905–1938), are particularly associated with spread of this devotion. Normally, the indulgence attached to the prayer *Iesu dulcissime, cuius effusa* (*Most sweet Jesus, overflowing*), which may be recited at any time, is partial, but if the prayer is recited publicly on the Feast of the Sacred Heart of Jesus (the Friday following the Second Sunday after Pentecost) the indulgence offered is plenary under the usual conditions. An image of the Sacred Heart need not be present, but is certainly to be encouraged.

Act of Contrition.[52] A partial indulgence is offered to the faithful who make an Act of Contrition using any approved formulas. Moreover, the pious recitation of certain psalms, especially the "Penitential Psalms"[53] or the "Gradual Psalms,"[54] satisfies this indulgence. In particular, Psalm 130 [129], *De Profundis* (Out of the Depths), or Psalm 51 [50], *Miserere* (Have mercy on me), are especially recommended. In practice, one will likely want to make an examination of conscience, which is indulgenced in the first part of this grant (discussed elsewhere), but it is not strictly required to do so.

The Marian Rosary.[55] Although, strictly speaking, the Marian rosary consists of four sets of mysteries (Joyful, Luminous, Sorrowful, and Glorious) and each set of mysteries is in turn comprised of five decades

---

51. *Actus reparationis* [*Sacrissimo Cordi Iesu*]. Enchiridion 1999, conc. 3; Enchiridion 1986, conc. 26. See also Raccolta, no. 256.

52. *Examen conscientiae et actus contritionis.* Enchiridion 1999, conc. 9, 2°; Enchiridion 1986, conc. 2 (Act of Contrition, which had then to be associated with at least one of three Acts of Theological Virtues); no. 19 (Psalm 130 [129], *De Profundis*); and no. 33 (Psalm 51 [50], *Miserere*). See also Raccolta, nos. 36 and 686.

53. The main Penitential Psalms are: 6; 32 (31); 38 (37); 51 (50); 102 (101); 130 (129); and 143 (142).

54. The Gradual Psalms (so named because they seem to have been sung by Jewish pilgrims as they made their way up the gradient toward Jerusalem) are Psalms 120 (119)–134 (133).

55. *Preces ad Beatissimam Virginem Mariam.* Enchiridion 1999, conc. 17 § 1, 1°; Enchiridion 1986, conc. 48. See also Raccolta, no. 395.

commemorating events within those mysteries, it is common for the term "Rosary" to be applied to the prayerful recitation of any one set of mysteries, that is, to the praying of just five decades, instead of twenty.[56]

A plenary indulgence under the usual conditions is offered to the faithful who pray the Marian Rosary[57] in a church or oratory, in a family gathering, within a religious Community or recognized association of the faithful, or in any other context in which the faithful have come together for an upright purpose. Moreover, if only five decades are prayed (as opposed to all twenty being said), those five decades must be prayed continuously, that is, without notable interruptions,[58] vocal prayer must accompany meditation on the mystery as they occur, and if the recitation is public, the mysteries must be announced.[59]

---

56. Prayers traditionally associated with the Rosary include the *Apostles' Creed*, the *Our Father*, the *Hail Mary*, the *Glory Be*, and the *Hail Holy Queen*, although, beyond the inclusion of the *Our Father* and *Hail Mary*, the precise make-up of the Rosary varies with time and place. See W. Hinnebusch, "Rosary", *New Catholic Encyclopedia* (New York: McGraw-Hill, 1967), vol. 12, pp. 667–670. It is, moreover, a common practice in many places to add, especially at the end of decades, additional prayers such as the "Fatima Prayer." These more recent additions may be included or not, as circumstances suggest, without impact on the indulgence.

57. The Marian rosary indulgenced here is that promoted by the Dominicans, but there are a number of other devotions identified as "rosaries," including ones promoted by the Franciscans, the Carmelites (the Brigittine rosary), the Rosary of the Seven Sorrows, rosaries in honor of the Holy Spirit or various saints, and so on. These other forms of rosaries are not indulgenced by this grant. Praying these other types of rosaries might be indulgenced under, say, Enchiridion 1999, conc. 15 or 21.

58. This is contrary to the rule in Raccolta, no. 395, Note 1, which allowed decades to be separated, provided the whole was completed on the same day. The elimination of this flexibility in the performance of the action is regrettable. Many lay persons (especially in a family setting) for whom the Rosary is an important devotional exercise simply cannot be sure of having sufficient uninterrupted time in which to say a complete Rosary (whether of five decades, or of twenty). The insistence on praying complete rosaries in a single session, while helpful in fostering reflection on the mysteries being prayed, does not seem designed to combat a serious spiritual flaw (such as might be occasioned by attempting in fits and starts the praying of the major hours of the Liturgy of the Hours) and can lead to scrupulosity among those wanting to use the Rosary for an indulgence. Some people deliberately break the Rosary into parts to be completed on the same day (say, two or three decades during one's morning commute, and two or three decades in one's return trip, or again, the praying the Sorrowful Mysteries on Good Friday morning, with each decade separated by an hour's worth of spiritual reading or other activities) and seem reasonable in so doing. Even under the current discipline, of course, short interruptions in prayer would seem insufficient to break up the "moral unity" of the Rosary for purposes of the indulgence. Nevertheless, some reconsideration of the implications of setting the norm as strictly as it now reads might be in order.

59. It is not expressly required that one hold rosary beads during this prayer, as was commonly set down under some earlier norms. Using such an object of devotion, however, surely contributes to the disposition of those seeking the indulgence attached to the Rosary, as well as serving practical purposes of good order.

For purposes of the indulgence, any set(s) of mysteries may be prayed on any day, but one would want to keep in mind the liturgical season when selecting which mysteries to pray and avoid, for example, praying the Sorrowful Mysteries on Christmas Day, or the Glorious Mysteries on Good Friday.

Prayer to Saint Joseph.[60] A partial indulgence is offered to the faithful who devoutly recite any approved prayer to Saint Joseph. A common formula is the *Ad te beate Ioseph* (*To thee, O blessed Joseph*).

Litanies.[61] The earliest use of litanies in the Church dates to her first centuries, when litanies accompanied liturgical processions. While litanies still occur in liturgical contexts (for example, the *Kyrie* at Mass), the prayerful content and character of many litanies has helped them to move out of strictly liturgical applications and into other areas of Christian spirituality. A partial indulgence is granted to those faithful who piously recite any approved litany. While any litany approved by competent ecclesiastical authority suffices for the purposes of this indulgence, certain litanies are especially recommended, namely, *Ss.mi Nominis Iesu* (Litany of the Most Holy Name), *Sacr.mi Cordis Iesu* (Litany of the Most Sacred Heart), *Pretiosissimi Sanguinis D.N. I.C.* (Litany of the Most Precious Blood of Our Lord Jesus Christ), *B. Mariae V.* (Litany of the Most Blessed Virgin Mary, or the Litany of Loreto), *S. Ioseph* (Litany of Saint Joseph), and *Sanctorum* (Litany of the Saints). For purposes of the indulgence, litanies may be recited by an individual anywhere, but they are more appropriate when prayed in union with others.

Little Offices.[62] The Divine Office, now more descriptively known as the Liturgy of the Hours, is the Church's formal way of observing the

---

60. *Preces in honorem S. Joseph.* Enchiridion 1999, conc. 19; Enchiridion 1986, conc. 6. See also Raccolta, no. 476. Circumstances might also suggest the use of the "Blessing of St. Joseph's Table" contained in the *Book of Blessings*, Chap. 53; *Shorter Book of Blessings*, Chap. 33, which would clearly satisfy the indulgence requirements.

61. *Preces novendiales, litaniae et parva Officia.* Enchiridion 1999, conc. 22, 2°; Enchiridion 1986, conc. 29. See also Raccolta, no. 114 (Holy Name of Jesus); 245 (Sacred Heart); 319 (Loretto); 462 (St. Joseph); and 687 (All Saints).

62. *Preces novendiales, litaniae et parva Officia.* Enchiridion 1999, conc. 22, 3°; Enchiridion 1986, conc. 36. See also Raccolta, no. 190 (Passion of Our Lord); no. 244 (Sacred Heart); no. 318 (Blessed Virgin Mary); no. 360 (Immaculate Conception); no. 461 (St. Joseph).

Lord's precept to pray without ceasing (Luke 18:1). The partial indulgence described in this grant, however, refers not to the Liturgy of the Hours, but instead to those prayers that came to be known as "Little Offices." Originally intended as a less-demanding substitute for the major exercises of the Divine Office, the so-called little offices lent themselves to use by lay persons especially before the reform of the Liturgy of the Hours subsequent to the Second Vatican Council. Notwithstanding the post-conciliar reforms of the Liturgy of the Hours, these little offices are still of value to many people in their personal spiritual life, and they are enriched by this indulgence.

Among the legitimately approved Little Offices (again, any of which suffice for this indulgence), the following are especially recommended: *Passionis D.N.I.C.* (Passion of Our Lord Jesus Christ), *Sacr.mi Cordis Iesu* (Most Sacred Heart of Jesus), *B. Mariae V.* (Blessed Virgin Mary), *Immaculatae Conceptionis* (Immaculate Conception), and *S. Ioseph* (Saint Joseph).

Pious Recitation of the Creed.[63] Either the *Apostles' Creed* (as used typically in the Marian Rosary) or the *Nicene-Constantinopolitan Creed* (as used most often in Mass) may be prayed for a partial indulgence. Praying a *Creed* when required for certain indulgences attached to visits to churches or oratories is not separately indulgenced.

Acts of Faith, Hope, and Charity.[64] A partial indulgence is offered to those faithful who recite the Acts of Faith, Hope, and Charity, using any approved formula.

Office for the Dead.[65] Praying *Lauds* (Morning Prayer) or *Vespers* (Evening Prayer) from the Liturgy of the Hours' Office for the Dead

---

63. *Professio Fidei et actus virtutum theologalium.* Enchiridion 1999, conc. 28 § 2, 3°; Enchiridion 1986, conc. 16.

64. *Professio Fidei et actus virtutum theologalium.* Enchiridion 1999, conc. 28 § 2, 4°; Enchiridion 1986, conc. 2, (wherein the individual Acts each satisfied for an indulgence, but the prayers needed to be joined to an Act of Contrition). See also Raccolta, no. 36. Given the long-standing practice offering indulgences for each of the Acts individually, and the lack of a clear requirement in the current grant to limit the indulgences only to those occasions wherein all three Acts are prayed together, it seems that each of the Acts is still separately indulged.

65. *Pro fidelibus defunctis.* Enchiridion 1999, conc. 29 § 2, 2°; Enchiridion 1986, conc. 18 (wherein the indulgence was not limited to the poor souls in Purgatory). See also Raccolta, no. 584 (wherein the indulgence could be retained by the one praying). Today the indulgences available under this grant may be applied only to the poor souls in Purgatory.

obtains for the faithful departed, and only for the faithful departed, a partial indulgence.[66] As we have seen elsewhere, while any indulgence may be offered for the dead, a few, including that offered here, can only be applied to the poor souls in Purgatory.

Specific Activities for the Faithful

A variety of activities that can be undertaken at the instigation of the faithful (and in which respect they differ from special occasions, discussed below, that are under the control of ecclesiastical leadership) are the subject of indulgences today. While earlier collections of indulgences listed many such works, far fewer prayers are indulgenced today, their number being limited to those that have a special history of devotional use by Christians over time. Unless indicated otherwise, all of these indulgences are partial, to be obtained under the usual circumstances for partial indulgences.[67] The indulgences discussed here follow the order in which they are presented in the Enchiridion 1999. Earlier comments about the use of objects of devotion in pursuing these indulgences should be borne in mind, although many of the actions indulgenced here tend to lend themselves less to the use of such objects than do indulgences attached to prayers.

Act of Family Consecration.[68] This indulgence is new with the Enchiridion 1999, though it was found in the Raccolta. It recognizes that the family is both the basic unit of society, and is also, as the Second Vatican Council put it, drawing on a long tradition of theological reflections on the family, a "domestic Church."[69] At the same

---

66. As noted elsewhere, this grant (which is combined with a partial indulgence attached to the prayer "Eternal rest") seems a good case in which to recall that the worth of partial indulgences depends, in part, on the intrinsic merit of the prayer or action undertaken. Obviously, to offer Morning or Evening Prayer for the dead is a more substantial undertaking than would be offering the simple prayer "Eternal rest," and in that regard it would be of greater benefit to the poor souls. On the other hand, "Eternal rest," being shorter, can be said more frequently for the faithful departed than can prayers from the Liturgy of the Hours.

67. Enchiridion 1999, Norm 17; Enchiridion 1986, Norm 20.

68. *Actus consecrationis familiarum.* Enchiridion 1999, conc. 1. See also Raccolta, no. 705. This act of consecration goes beyond the praiseworthy "Blessings of a Family" contained in the *Book of Blessings*, Chap. 1; *Shorter Book of Blessings*, Chap. 1. Devotions toward the Sacred Heart were extensive in the Raccolta, nos. 223 ff. For devotions oriented to the Holy Family, see Raccolta, nos. 273–276.

69. Vatican Council II, const. *Lumen gentium* no. 11.

time, family life is under attack from a wide variety of quarters today and needs ever more the protection of God to survive in this present era of secularism.

To obtain this plenary indulgence (under the usual conditions) a family[70] is to gather before an image of the Sacred Heart of Jesus or of the Holy Family and, with the assistance of a priest or deacon if possible, consecrate itself in honor of the Sacred Heart or Holy Family, using any formularies approved for this use. On the anniversary of this initial consecration, a family renewing its consecration obtains a partial indulgence.

***Teaching and Learning Christian Doctrine.*[71]** A partial indulgence is offered to those who engage in teaching or learning Christian doctrine.[72] Besides the obvious application of this indulgence in traditional classroom settings of all age and ability levels, the indulgence applies to self-study, and thus to personal reading, listening to live or recorded lectures, watching videos on doctrine, and so on. No minimum amount of time is currently specified for obtaining the indulgence, but one might wish to keep in mind as guides that indulgences attached to Scripture reading or to adoration of the Blessed Sacrament specify minimum time periods of a half hour, and consider those.

---

70. For purposes of defining the "family" here, besides the nuclear family actually participating, one should include nuclear family members whose absence cannot be avoided without serious inconvenience, and members of the extended family who reside with the nuclear family and who wish to associate themselves with the consecration. If for some reason a given member of the family does not obtain the indulgence (say because of insufficient disposition), the indulgence would still be applicable to others. As is the case with all indulgences, this one may be applied by suffrage to the dead, and deceased members of the family would seem especially worthy of remembrance.

71. *Doctrina christiana*. Enchiridion 1999, conc. 6; Enchiridion 1986, conc. 20. See also Raccolta, no. 693 (specifying a minimum of twenty minutes). Circumstances might also suggest the use of "Blessing of Students and Teachers" contained in the *Book of Blessings*, Chap. 5; *Shorter Book of Blessings*, Chap. 4.

72. Christian doctrine is a much wider field than just, say, the catechism. It would include all of the major ecclesiastical disciplines (theology, Scripture, canon law, Church history, and so on) and many other subjects where discussions of good morals or religion are an issue. (See 1983 CIC 827). At the same time, one may not so expand the notion of doctrine as to include virtually anything of interest to Christians. For example, the study of Hindu philosophy might be interesting, and perhaps even useful to a Christian apologist, but it would not be the subject of this indulgence. Also, while the indulgence probably envisions *Catholic* doctrine as the subject of this indulgence, *favores ampliari*, the study of any Christian doctrine that is not in conflict with Church teaching should suffice for the indulgence.

Adoration of the Blessed Sacrament.[73] The Blessed Sacrament is truly
the Body, Blood, Soul, and Divinity of Christ (CCC 1374). When
one is before the Blessed Sacrament, one is in the real and substantial
presence of Jesus, the Second Person of the Blessed Trinity. There one
has the privilege of worshipping him whose infinite merits are even
more richly poured out in the gift of indulgences. For this plenary
indulgence, besides the usual conditions, one's prayerful presence before
the Blessed Sacrament must be continued for at least a half hour.[74]
Numerous prayers lend themselves to use during these periods, but
none are strictly required for the indulgence.

Given the rules by which those who do not fulfill all the
requirements for a plenary indulgence may still obtain a partial one
for their efforts,[75] it is not really necessary to state that any visits to
the Blessed Sacrament, even those less than a half hour in length,
suffice for a partial indulgence; nevertheless, to underscore the great
benefits of Eucharistic adoration, the availability of a partial indulgence
for any such visits is expressly mentioned in the grant.[76] Note that if
one cannot be in the presence of the Eucharist at all, one can nevertheless seek the indulgence offered for a spiritual Communion.[77]

Special Hymns and Prayers in Honor of Blessed Sacrament.[78] A partial
indulgence is offered to those faithful who devoutly recite (or sing, as
the case may be) approved prayers or hymns in honor of the Blessed
Sacrament. Among the most renowned of such prayers and hymns are
Adoro Te devote (*Humbly we adore Thee*), *Tantum ergo* (*Down in adoration
falling*), and *O Sacrum Convivium* (*O Holy Feast*). These prayers and
hymns, ranking among the most beautiful works in Christian poetry,
are often encountered in Eucharistic exposition and Benediction rites,

---

73. *Eucharistica adoratio et processio.* Enchiridion 1999, conc. 7 § 1, 1°; Enchiridion 1986,
conc. 3.

74. The happy practice of parish Holy Hours is slowly making its return after several
decades of neglect. These represent an ideal opportunity to take advantage of this indulgence.
See also Raccolta, nos. 168–169.

75. See Enchiridion 1999, Norm 20 § 4; Enchiridion 1986, 23 § 4.

76. *Eucharistica adoratio et processio.* Enchiridion 1999, conc. 7 § 2, 1°; Enchiridion 1986,
conc. 3.

77. See Enchiridion 1999, Norm 8 § 2, 1°; Enchiridion 1986, conc. 15.

78. *Eucharistica adoratio et processio.* Enchiridion 1999, conc. 7 § 2, 2°; Enchiridion 1986,
conc. 4 (*Adoro Te devote*); 40 (*O Sacrum convivium*); and 59 (*Tantum ergo*). See also Raccolta,
nos. 165–166.

where they serve to augment the indulgences that already endow these holy actions.[79] Strictly speaking, however, there is no express requirement that, to benefit by the indulgences attached to these prayers and hymns, one must actually be in the presence of the Blessed Sacrament. In that regard, these prayers would seem suitable for an act of spiritual Communion.[80]

Spiritual Communion.[81] The Eucharist is the source and summit of the Christian life (CCC 1324; 1983 CIC 897). Those who cannot participate in the Eucharist are strongly encouraged to invite Jesus into their hearts in the special way known as "Spiritual Communion" and are offered a partial indulgence for so doing.[82] Many formulas for spiritual communions have been mentioned by the saints or can otherwise be imagined, beginning with something as simple as "Lord, please come to me spiritually in communion," but no specific phrases are required.

Post-Communion Prayer of Thanksgiving.[83] A partial indulgence is offered to those faithful who make a special act of thanksgiving to Our Lord for the gift of receiving him in the Eucharist. While this expression of gratitude can take a wide variety of forms, two prayers in particular are recommended, the *Anima Christi* (*Soul of Christ*) and the *En ego, o bone et dulcissime Iesu* (*Prayer before Crucifix*). The actual presence of a crucifix is not required for the gaining of this indulgence, but one may safely assume that this condition would be satisfied in most churches and oratories. Moreover, an image of Christ crucified may be used. Remember, too, that reception of the Eucharist is *not* required in order for one to fulfill, for example, one's Sunday obligation (1983 CIC 1247–1248). Therefore, those making such a special act of gratitude after

---

79. See Enchiridion 1999, conc. 7.

80. See Enchiridion 1999, conc. 8 § 2, 1°.

81. *Eucharistica et spiritualis communio.* Enchiridion 1999, conc. 8 § 2, 1°; Enchiridion 1986, conc. 15. See also Raccolta, no. 164.

82. There are no fast or abstinence requirements for spiritual communion such as are demanded for reception of the Eucharist in the Sacred Species (1983 CIC 919 § 1). A spiritual Communion does not satisfy the annual obligation of Catholics in this matter (1983 CIC 920) nor does it satisfy the reception of Communion requirement associated with plenary indulgences (Enchiridion 1999, Norm 20 § 2).

83. *Eucharistica et spiritualis communio.* Enchiridion 1999, conc. 8 § 2, 2°; Enchiridion 1986, conc. 10 (*Anima Christi*) and 22 (*En ego, o bone et dulcissime Iesu*). See also Raccolta, no. 131.

receiving Communion on such days are eligible for this indulgence, even though they are assisting at a Mass that is already required of them. Finally, note that, although receiving the Eucharist is a requirement of most plenary indulgences, there is no prior requirement to receive indulgences at all. Thus, strictly speaking, there is no formal requirement that a thanksgiving for Eucharistic reception be made (however much that observation might grate on pious ears). As a result, those making a thanksgiving for a Eucharist received as part of fulfilling the requirements for a plenary indulgence can also obtain this indulgence.

Examination of Conscience.[84] The Catholic Church wishes her members to grow in self-awareness, and over time to come to see themselves as Christ sees them, that is, in the fullness of his truth. An important aid in progressing toward self-mastery is the personal examination of conscience. The most common time of the day for an examination of conscience (which might last ten minutes or so) is just before bedtime, when the day's events are basically over, but not so remote in past that they cannot be recalled. Another common time for examination, though perhaps briefer, is around midday.

To encourage the practice of examining one's conscience, the Church offers a partial indulgence to the faithful who engage in this act of self-reflection in the light of Christ. This examination is especially encouraged prior to Confession and as such obviously makes good sense as an exercise that improves one's disposition to cooperate with the sacramental graces Christ offers in the Sacrament of Reconciliation. One would generally want to follow such an examination of conscience with an expression of sorrow for one's sins, say, by an Act of Contrition.[85]

Spiritual Exercises and Monthly Recollection.[86] A plenary indulgence under the usual conditions is available to the Christian faithful who spend at least three full days on spiritual exercises (also known as a

---

84. *Examen conscientiae et actus contritionis.* Enchiridion 1999, conc. 9, 1°. See also Raccolta, no. 690.

85. Enchiridion 1999, no. 9, 2°.

86. *Exercitia spiritalia et recollectio menstrua.* Enchiridion 1999, conc. 10; Enchiridion 1986, conc. 25 and 45. See also Raccolta, no. 689.

retreat). The grant of the indulgence makes clear that the days must be "full" (*integros*), so a weekend retreat with, say, arrival on Friday evening and departure on Sunday afternoon would not qualify for the plenary indulgence, however beneficial such retreats might be in others respects.[87] It should also be assumed that such a retreat must be guided, that is, it should be under the supervision of a retreat master or spiritual director. Personal quiet time away from the press of daily duties, even if it is time set aside for spiritual growth, would not qualify as a retreat in the sense of this grant.

A partial indulgence is also offered to those who participate in a monthly period of recollection. No minimum amount of time is specified for the recollection period,[88] but one should assume that time must somehow be supervised, lest it essentially amount to a period of personal prayer. One should try, but is not strictly required, to attend such sessions each and every month for the indulgence. Otherwise, frequent absences would make less cogent the claim that one is really engaged in a *monthly* period of recollection, as opposed to an occasional period of recollection.

Stations of the Cross.[89] A plenary indulgence under the usual conditions is offered to the faithful[90] who undertake to make the Stations of the Cross (on their own or in a group, under the leadership of a cleric or not).[91] Some additional requirements—and options—apply in the case of this indulgence:

---

87. The retreats described here might qualify for a partial indulgence, under, say, Enchiridion 1999, nos. 15 and 16, as well as under the usual rules for the acquisition of partial indulgences in Enchiridion 1999, Norm 20 § 4.

88. One might recall, though, the half-hour minimum period required for indulgences attached to adoration of the Blessed Sacrament and reading of Sacred Scripture and use that time as a guide. On the other hand, the indulgence attached to meditation on the Passion of the Our Lord suggests, under certain circumstances, only 15 minutes. See note 5 of this grant.

89. *In memoria Passionis et Mortis Domini.* Enchiridion 1999, conc. 13; Enchiridion 1986, 63. Also called "Via Crucis," and "Via Dolorosa." See also Raccolta, no. 194.

90. This is one the few Specific Grant indulgences that makes special mention of Eastern-rite faithful. Because, as is noted in the concession itself, the pious exercise of the Stations of the Cross is not common among Eastern Christians, they may obtain the plenary indulgence associated with the Stations of the Cross by participating in any devotional exercise related to the Passion of Our Lord as established by their own ecclesiastical leaders.

91. It is not required that these Stations be performed on Good Friday, or even on Fridays of Lent. But for liturgical reasons, given the Church's week-long celebration of Easter, it would not be appropriate to make the Stations of the Cross on, say, Friday of Easter Week.

1. The Stations themselves must have been legitimately erected, that is, a private set of stations set up on individual authority would not suffice. This norm helps guard against the intrusion of unduly idiosyncratic elements in the devotion, as could more likely occur if ecclesiastical authority were not involved in the establishment of a set of stations.
2. The stations must be 14 in number, though they need not contain images or representations of the specific events they represent.[92]
3. Simple meditation on Passion of Our Lord in general is sufficient during the stations. In other words, while it is beneficial to meditate upon the specific event depicted in each station, it is not strictly required for the indulgence to apply, nor need any set words be used to express the meditations, although the use of legitimately approved formulas is encouraged.
4. Generally, one must move from station to station. In the case of a larger group of faithful making the stations together, however, it suffices that a leader move from station to station while the faithful participate from their places. The leader need not be a cleric, but obviously if one is available, it contributes to the sign value of the Stations.
5. If persons are unable to make the Stations (for reasons beyond simply inconvenience) they may obtain the same indulgence by spending time (15 minutes is suggested) in devotional reading or meditation on the Passion of Our Lord.[93]
6. Local ecclesiastical authority can substitute another pious exercise for the traditional Stations of the Cross for purposes of the same indulgence that is attached to the Stations, provided that the

---

92. Over the centuries, the number of the stations has varied from just a few to over thirty. The present form of fourteen stations dates, however, back to the sixteenth century and seems to be pastorally effective. The sometime recent practice of adding a fifteenth station (namely, the Resurrection) does not affect the indulgence, and a fifteenth station may be used or omitted as circumstances suggest.

93. Scriptural accounts of the Passion of Our Lord seem especially suitable here but are not required. Note that the character of the reading must be devotional. Thus, say, scientific analyses of the Crucifixion, or narrative books about holy sites associated with the Passion of Our Lord, however moving such materials might be, would not suffice for purposes of this indulgence.

substituted exercise is similarly focused on the Passion and Death of Our Lord.[94]

Moreover, a plenary indulgence under the usual conditions is offered to the faithful who devoutly follow by live television or radio the Pope as he leads the Stations of the Cross in Rome, typically on Good Friday.

Special Use of Objects of Piety.[95] Objects of piety, when used to help one direct the heart and mind to God, are a worthy part of a healthy spiritual life. These objects come in a wide variety of forms: rosaries, medals, crucifixes, holy figures and pictures, relics, and so on.[96] Besides the partial indulgence attached to the use of objects of devotion,[97] a plenary indulgence under the usual conditions is offered to the faithful who make use of such objects under certain conditions, namely, when, on the feast of Saints Peter and Paul (June 29), and using an object of piety that was blessed by the pope or a bishop,[98] the faithful lift their prayers to God and add a Profession of Faith according to any approved formula.[99]

---

94. If the character of the substituted exercise differs notably from those associated with the Stations, it is possible that such exercises would yet serve for the indulgences attached to the use of objects of devotion (Enchiridion 1999, conc. 14 § 2 or even Enchiridion 1999, General Grant, conc. 3), though in such cases the indulgence offered is a partial one, not the plenary one offered for the Stations of the Cross.

95. *Obiectorum pietatis usus.* Enchiridion 1999, conc. 14 § 1; Enchiridion 1986, conc. 35. Blessings for objects, large or small, that are intended to foster the devotion of the faithful are contained in the *Book of Blessings*, Part III and IV; *Shorter Book of Blessings*, Part III.

96. A Bible is not expressly listed among the examples of items that may be considered as objects of devotion, but it seems that a strong case can be made for its inclusion. The many gestures of respect made toward the Sacred Scriptures in, for example, liturgical contexts suggest that such reverence is also not out of place in private settings. Many families, for example, do not simply have a copy of the Bible in their homes, but have the Scriptures set up in a dignified place. Moreover, holding onto a Bible or kissing it during, say, the renewal of one's baptismal vows on the anniversary of one's baptism day (Enchiridion 1999, conc. 28 § 2, 1°) would seem entirely appropriate in such settings.

97. See Enchiridion 1999, conc. 14 § 2.

98. This indulgence is to underscore the principle of unity that the pope and bishops represent in a unique way within the Church. Objects blessed by priests and deacons are of real value in the spiritual life, of course, though they do not suffice for this plenary indulgence. See instead norms for the general use of objects of devotion in Enchiridion 1999, conc. 14 § 2.

99. Formulas that would certainly be acceptable here would include the Apostles' Creed, The Nicene Creed, and the Renewal of Baptismal Vows from the Easter Vigil. Slightly longer, but well worth considering, is the "Credo of the People of God," composed by Pope Paul VI and published on June 30, 1968. The actual profession of faith begins a dozen or so paragraphs into the document.

Participation in Preaching Missions.[100] While not as common as in the past, sacred missions are usually held at the parish level, and consist of an invitation (usually to a priest[101]) to visit the parish and make a series of addresses for the spiritual edification of the parishioners and others who wish to attend. A plenary indulgence under the usual conditions is offered to the faithful who, having devoutly attended at least some of the special sermons, also attend the formal conclusion of the mission. One need not be a member of the parish (or diocese, if the mission is held at that level) to benefit by this indulgence. More generally, a partial indulgence is offered to the faithful whenever they attentively and devoutly listen to preaching of the Word of God.[102]

Prayers in Honor of Newly Canonized or Beatified Persons.[103] To foster the veneration of newly canonized or beatified persons, a plenary indulgence under the usual conditions is offered to the faithful who, within one year of the elevation of the saints or blessed, attend in a church or oratory solemn services in their honor, and pray there an *Our Father* and a *Creed*. A partial indulgence is offered to those faithful under the same circumstances as above, but without requiring that a service in honor of the newly canonized or beatified person be conducted.

The Sign of the Cross.[104] The most universally recognized gesture of Catholics is the Sign of the Cross. A partial indulgence is offered to those who make the Sign of the Cross reverently while pronouncing the words of the blessing, that is, the formula in honor of the Trinity ("In the name of the Father, and of the Son, and of the Holy Spirit. Amen"). When we as Catholics make this gesture that recalls the death of Christ on the Cross and recite the same words that Christ told us to use for Baptism, we are recalling that our Baptism brought

---

100. *Praedicationis sacrae participatio.* Enchiridion 1999, conc. 16; Enchiridion 1986, conc. 41. See also Raccolta, nos. 633–634, 692.

101. While not permitted to give homilies in the liturgy, lay persons can engage in preaching, even within churches and oratories, and might be legitimately invited to give such missions as described herein. See 1983 CIC 766.

102. As is to be expected, merely paying attention to homilies at Sunday Mass, being already required of the faithful as part of their Sunday Mass obligation, does not suffice for the partial indulgence outlined here.

103. *Preces in honorem aliorum Sanctorum necnon Beatorum.* Enchiridion 1999, conc. 21 § 2.

104. *Professio Fidei et actus virtutum theologalium.* Enchiridion 1999, conc. 28 § 2, 2°; Enchiridion 1986, conc. 55. See also Raccolta, no. 678.

us into the death of Jesus and made us heirs to the merits he won for us by his Passion, Death, and Resurrection.

Visit to a cemetery.[105] Any devout visit to a cemetery, accompanied by any prayers (including mental ones[106]) for the dead suffices for this partial indulgence, which is applicable *only* to the dead. Those for whom one might wish to apply the indulgence thereby obtained need not be buried in the cemetery visited.

Reading Sacred Scripture.[107] The Church's desire to see more people reading the Sacred Scriptures for spiritual growth and nourishment (CCC 131–133) is reflected in this grant of a plenary or partial indulgence for reading the Bible. The grant is plenary under the usual conditions if, using one of the many versions of Scripture approved by ecclesiastical authority, and with the veneration due to the Word of God, the faithful spend at least a half hour in spiritual reading of the Bible, whether Old Testament or New. If the amount of time spent is less, the indulgence is partial. In an interesting expansion over the earlier grant of this indulgence, the Enchiridion 1999 adds that, should one be unable to read the Bible for various reasons, then the grant of the indulgence applies as above for listening to the Word of God, either live or via recordings.[108]

Special Occasions or Events for the Faithful

Certain special events or unique occasions in life have been favored with indulgences to help those celebrating or participating in them to appreciate more deeply their significance and to benefit more specially

---

105. *Pro fidelibus defunctis.* Enchiridion 1999, conc. 29 § 2, 1°; Enchiridion 1986, conc. 13. Note that the indulgences available under this grant may be applied only to the poor souls in Purgatory. See also Raccolta, no. 592.

106. One might want to use, however, the special prayers for visiting a cemetery that are provided in the *Book of Blessings*, Chapter 57; *Shorter Book of Blessings*, Chapter 35.

107. *Sacrae Scripturae lectio.* Enchiridion 1999, conc. 30; Enchiridion 1986, conc. 50. See also Raccolta, no. 694 (wherein only a quarter of an hour was required for a partial indulgence).

108. This expansion seems little more than an occasion wherein was exercised the principle of *favores ampliari*, for the expansion applies to the manner of fulfilling the requirement of the indulgence, and did not modify the requirement itself, say, by substituting readings from the *Lives of the Saints* for those unable to read the Scriptures.

from marking them.[109] While earlier collections of indulgences listed more such works and events, those that are indulgenced today reflect a special history of devotional use by Christians over time. The indulgences discussed here follow the order in which they are presented in the Enchiridion 1999, except that three indulgences, namely the Divine Mercy Sunday indulgence, those offered for certain Eastern Prayers, and the indulgence offered at the time of death, are discussed at the end of section due to their special characters.[110] Earlier comments about the use of objects of devotion in pursuing these indulgences should be borne in mind, although these actions tend to lend themselves less to the use of such objects than do indulgences attached to prayers.

Papal Blessings.[111] The papal blessing described here, which results in a plenary indulgence under the usual conditions, is the special blessing designated as "ad Urbem et Orbem," or "Urbi et Orbi," or "to the City [of Rome] and to the World." Typically, this is the blessing that the pope offers from his window on Sundays or after a Wednesday *Angelus*, or on special occasions such as Christmas or Easter. The pope himself, or commentators on the scene, will identify when the blessing being offered is "to the City and the World." Even if they fail to mention the fact of the indulgence, it applies if the blessing is "Urbi et Orbi." Those accepting this blessing, even by means of electronic broadcast,[112] show their desire for union with the Successor of Peter. The pious

---

109. Indeed, Enchiridion 1999, Introduction no. 3, expressly notes that some indulgences that might at first glance appear to enrich the celebration of Mass are actually intended to underscore the special character of the specific event in question. See, e.g., Enchiridion 1999 for indulgences attached to First Communion (conc. 8 § 1, 1°), First Mass by a priest (conc. 27 § 1), and Mass at the Conclusion of a Eucharistic Congress (conc. 7 § 1, 4°).

110. A special event not listed in the post-conciliar Enchiridions, but enriched with indulgences since the fourteenth century, is the quarter-century mark, known as the Jubilee or Holy Year indulgences. See Hagedorn, p. 38. The next such indulgence will presumably occur in 2025.

111. *Benedictio papalis.* Enchiridion 1999, conc. 4; Enchiridion 1986, conc. 12. See also Raccolta, no. 695.

112. The papal blessing broadcast must be live, so tape recordings or journalistic accounts of the blessing do not suffice either for the indulgence or, for that matter, for the reception of the blessing itself. At the same time, though, some aspects of modern, world-wide communications still need to be examined. For example, many "live" broadcasts are, strictly-speaking, tape-delayed transmissions and the time-delay that seems appropriate for certain broadcasts originating in Rome but intended for audiences in other parts of the world should be considered. *Favores ampliari,* I am inclined to think that "live" broadcasts that are time-delayed for transmission at locally-equivalent times should be considered sufficient for purposes of acquiring an

acceptance of any other blessings by the pope is certainly a praiseworthy action, but is not enriched by an indulgence.

There is another way to obtain the plenary indulgence attached to papal "Urbi et Orbi" blessings, namely, at the hands of diocesan bishops. Three times a year, at Masses celebrated with special solemnity and so designated by the bishop, the faithful in attendance at such a Mass may obtain, under the usual conditions, the plenary indulgence described here.[113] There is, as yet at least, no provision for those following such local events electronically to receive the indulgence attached thereto.

Finally, the apostolic blessing at the time of death,[114] which can be administered by priests, is yet a third way to obtain this indulgence. For a discussion of the special features of this manner of receiving the indulgence, see below.

***Days Dedicated Universally to Promoting Religious Ends.*[115]** From time to time, the Holy See dedicates a certain day or series of days to the promotion of a specific religious value such as encouraging vocations, supporting marriage, aiding youth in the faith, meeting the needs of the sick or disabled, and so on. The faithful who participate in some special activity related to these goals may obtain a plenary indulgence thereby, under the usual conditions. Such activities might be attendance at a prayer rally or lecture dedicated to the theme. But, while the specific activity might be organized locally, it must be dedicated to the themes as set out by the Holy See. In other words, a diocesan rally for some worthy cause, while certainly deserving of support, is not the subject of an indulgence here.[116] Engaging in personal prayer for these universal intentions suffices for a partial indulgence, but merely recall-

---

indulgence that might be attached to such events. Virtually all of these would be broadcast locally within 24 hours of their original celebration in Rome.

113. Enchiridion 1999, Norm 7, 2°.

114. Enchiridion 1999, conc. 12.

115. *Dies ad aliquem religiosum finem celebrandum universaliter dicatae.* Enchiridion 1999, conc. 5; Enchiridion 1986, conc. 37 (wherein only prayers for the promotion of priestly and religious vocations were mentioned).

116. It might be an apt subject of a partial indulgence declared under episcopal authority. See Enchiridion 1999, Norm 7, 1°.

ing the promotion of these ends in, say, the intention at Sunday Mass would not suffice for obtain the plenary indulgence.[117]

Solemn Reposition of the Blessed Sacrament on Holy Thursday.[118]
At the conclusion of the Evening Mass of the Lord's Supper on Holy Thursday, the Blessed Sacrament is removed from its usual tabernacle and is solemnly reposed on a special altar. The main tabernacle is left open and empty until the Easter Vigil so that Catholics experience something of what the disciples of the Lord must have felt when Jesus was taken from them soon after the Last Supper. Any Catholic with a lively sense of the Real Presence of Jesus in the tabernacle recognizes the odd feeling of emptiness that arises when Our Lord is no longer really and substantially present in our churches. A plenary indulgence under the usual conditions is offered to those faithful who during the Rite of Transfer sing together or simply even pray alone the Eucharistic hymn *Tantum ergo* (Down in Adoration Falling). Participation in the procession to the Altar of Repose augments one's disposition here, but is not strictly required for this indulgence. Such action is, under current norms, separately indulgenced (see below).

Eucharistic Procession.[119] A plenary indulgence under the usual conditions is offered to those faithful who devoutly take part in a Eucharistic Procession, whether the procession stays inside the church or moves outside. Such processions are most commonly held on the Feast of the Body and Blood of Christ (on the Thursday after Trinity Sunday, sometimes simply called *Corpus Christi*). Participation in a procession held on that day is encouraged, but any public Eucharistic procession suffices for obtaining this indulgence. Certainly, procession to the Altar of Repose on Holy Thursday would be an indulgenced activity.

---

117. This is so not only because simply praying for the intention does not suffice for the plenary indulgence under the tenor of the grant, but also because, as we have noted before, indulgences are not offered to one who is performing an action already required by law or precept (Enchiridion 1999, Norm 21 § 1), as would be the case for someone joining in the Prayers of the Faithful at Sunday Mass.

118. *Eucharistica adoratio et procession.* Enchiridion 1999, conc. 7 § 1, 2°; Enchiridion 1986, conc. 59. See also Raccolta, no. 145.

119. *Eucharistica adoratio et processio.* Enchiridion 1999, conc. 7 § 1, 3°. See also Raccolta, no. 150.

Eucharistic Congress.[120] A plenary indulgence under the usual conditions is offered to those faithful who devoutly take part in the solemn concluding rites of a Eucharistic Congress. International congresses are well-advertised and are held in various countries, but regional and even local Eucharistic congresses also qualify for this indulgence. Personal presence at the concluding rites is required for the plenary indulgence, but following the proceedings by broadcast would doubtless suffice for a partial indulgence.

First Communion.[121] Individuals making their First Communion, regardless of their age, and those faithful who devoutly assist at such ceremonies, are offered a plenary indulgence under the usual conditions.[122] Although First Communions are now usually celebrated at Mass, such a setting is not strictly required to benefit by this indulgence. Also, in light of the principle *favores ampliari*, this indulgence might depart somewhat from the usual rule about indulgences not being available to those who are required to perform certain actions anyway. For example, an adult convert might make his or her First Communion at a regular Sunday Mass that others are obligated to attend, or perhaps at the Easter Vigil. Even though others in the congregation might be fulfilling thereby their Mass attendance obligation, if they unite themselves in a particular way to the Church's joy that another of her sons or daughters is receiving Jesus for the first time in Holy Communion, they would benefit by the indulgence.

Eucharistic Devotion on Penitential Fridays.[123] Fridays in the penitential season of Lent are privileged times in which to meditate on the Passion of Our Lord (1983 CIC 1250–1251) and Good Friday is the most solemn day of penance in the Church year. On Fridays in Lent and on Good Friday, the Church makes available a plenary indulgence,

---

120. *Eucharistica adoratio et processio.* Enchiridion 1999, conc. 7 § 1, 4°; Enchiridion 1986, conc. 23. See also Raccolta, no. 602.

121. *Eucharistica et spiritualis communio.* Enchiridion 1999, conc. 8 § 1, 1°; Enchiridion 1986, conc. 42. See also Raccolta, no. 151.

122. Strictly speaking, others in attendance at a First Communion need not actually receive Communion at the same time, but since reception of the Eucharist is one of the requirements for a plenary indulgence anyway, it certainly seems appropriate to receive the Eucharist at the same time as the First Communicant.

123. *Eucharistica et spiritualis communio.* Enchiridion 1999, conc. 8 § 1, 2°; Enchiridion 1986, conc. 22.

under the usual conditions,[124] to those faithful who, having received Communion that day, recite the prayer *En ego, o bone et dulcissime Iesu* (O, Good and gentle Jesus) before an image of Jesus Christ crucified. It is better known as the "Prayer Before a Crucifix" and is one of the few prayers not known best by its opening words.

The image of the crucifixion can be a picture, a statue, an icon such as the twelfth Station of the Cross, or the crucifix near an altar or on a rosary. But one should keep in mind that a plain cross or other more abstract representation of the Crucifixion would not satisfy the requirement for this plenary indulgence. Holy Communion may be received at any time on the Friday, but it must precede the offering of the *En ego, o bone et dulcissime Iesu*.

Participation in Week-of-Christian-Unity Events.[125] Activities to promote Christian unity are usually observed January 18–25, though other dates (especially around Pentecost) are sometimes selected for particular reasons. A plenary indulgence under the usual conditions is offered to the Christian faithful who participate in any related functions during the designated week, provided they also take part in the closing functions.

Veneration of the Cross on Good Friday.[126] A plenary indulgence under the usual conditions is offered to the faithful who take part in Good Friday services, specifically, the solemn veneration of the Cross.

Papal Rosary.[127] A plenary indulgence under the usual conditions is offered to the faithful who join by live television or radio broadcast with the pope as he leads the Rosary.[128]

---

124. Because this indulgence itself requires reception of Holy Communion, an additional reception of the Eucharist within the usual allotted period of time is not required.

125. *Hebdomada pro christianorum unitate.* Enchiridion 1999, conc. 11 § 1. See also Raccolta, no. 622.

126. *In memoria Passionis et Mortis Domini.* Enchiridion 1999, conc. 13, 1°; Enchiridion 1986, conc. 17.

127. *Preces ad Beatissimam Virginem Mariam.* Enchiridion 1999, conc. 17 § 1, 2°.

128. As discussed elsewhere, *favores ampliari*, it seems reasonable that this indulgence is also obtained by those following the event live on the Internet by a "Web cast," but recordings are not sufficient either by the tenor of the grant (*dum a Summo Pontifice peragitur*) or by past interpretations of similar grants. See, e.g., *Canon Law Digest* III: 390.

***Saints Day Prayers.*[129]** A partial indulgence is available to the faithful who offer any approved prayer in honor of a saint (such as those prayers found in the Roman Missal or in Liturgy of the Hours) on the saint's feast day.[130]

***Novenas.*[131]** The practice of praying for specific intentions over nine days draws its model from the example of the Apostles and Our Lady during the nine days that passed from the Ascension of Our Lord to the coming of the Holy Spirit at Pentecost (Acts 1:12–14). A partial indulgence is granted to those faithful who participate in public novenas such as are held before Christmas, Pentecost, or the feast of the Immaculate Conception (this listing being illustrative only, not exhaustive). The indulgence does not apply to private novenas, even if joined in by groups of faithful.[132]

***A Priest's First Mass and Certain Ordination Anniversaries.*[133]** In earlier times it was not uncommon for a priest to celebrate his first Mass alone or "privately" as the saying went. Today, most newly ordained priests celebrate their first Mass in the presence of a congregation, and in so doing they better reflect the public character of the Church's lit-

---

129. *Preces in honorem aliorum Sanctorum necnon Beatorum.* Enchiridion 1999, conc. 21 § 1; Enchiridion 1986, conc. 54.

130. This does not seem to be a case in which the argument of *favores ampliari* can be used to extend the indulgence to those offering prayers in honor of a Blessed (*beatus*) even though the distinctions between saints and *beati* are fewer than in times past, and even though in areas or within groups dedicated to *beati*, the differences between saints and *beati* are practically non-existent. The grant of this indulgence goes on to mention *beati* in § 2, and thereby suggests that if the Church had wanted to extend the indulgence in § 1 to *beati*, she could have easily done so. Thus the norm that indulgences must be strictly performed according to their tenor prevails over possible *favores ampliari* arguments. See also de Angelis, nos. 102–104.

131. *Preces novendiales, litaniae et parva Officia.* Enchiridion 1999, conc. 22, 1°; Enchiridion 1986, conc. 34. See also Raccolta, nos. 284 (Pentecost) and 361 (Immaculate Conception).

132. Such private novenas, however, might well be indulgenced under the terms of Enchiridion 1999, General Grant, conc. 4 or perhaps Specific Grant, conc. 15. Although in other cases I have argued that "public" connotes no need for ecclesiastical sanction or sponsorship, here I think the tenor of the grant does require such an official character to the novena. The restriction of the novena indulgence to public (that is, ecclesiastically authorized) novenas serves to underscore the bond of communion that each member of the faithful should foster with the whole Church, and perhaps to avoid endorsing novena intentions that are excessively individualistic or narrow.

133. *Prima sacerdotum Missa et iubilares Ordinationum celebrationes.* Enchiridion 1999, conc. 27; Enchiridion 1986, cons. 43 (*Prima Missa neosacerdotum*) and 49 (*Sacerdotalis Ordinationis celebrationes iubilares*). See also Raccolta, nos. 676 (those assisting at a first Mass) and 742 (the priest celebrating a first Mass).

urgy. As encouragement to a wider participation in this great moment, a plenary indulgence under the usual conditions is offered to both the priest celebrating and to the faithful participating, in whatever capacity, in a priest's first "public" or "scheduled" Mass, regardless of whether he might have already offered Mass once or more "privately."

With similar gratitude to God for the gift of many years in priestly ministry, a plenary indulgence is offered under the usual conditions to the priest and people celebrating the twenty-fifth, fiftieth, sixtieth, or seventieth anniversary of priestly (not diaconal) ordination wherein the priest renews his intention to fulfill his vocational duties faithfully. Additionally (and this is new in the Enchiridion 1999), to the bishop and people celebrating the twenty-fifth, fortieth, or fiftieth anniversary of episcopal ordination wherein the bishop renews his intention to fulfill his vocational duties faithfully, a plenary indulgence under the usual conditions is offered. Although it would be unusual these days for a priest or bishop to celebrate his ordination anniversary outside of Mass, strictly speaking, the grant of this indulgence distinguishes between the indulgence offered upon the formal renewal of vows by the priest and the indulgence arising from the participation in an anniversary Mass by the people. *Favores ampliari*, I believe this indulgence may be obtained by the priest or bishop and the people participating in either or both ceremonies.[134]

A Special Profession of Faith.[135] A plenary indulgence under the usual conditions is offered to the faithful upon the renewal of their baptismal vows during the Easter Vigil. This indulgence represents a slight departure from the usual rule that indulgences cannot be obtained by those who are fulfilling other legal duties.[136] Catholics are bound to attend Mass on Easter (as indeed they every Sunday), but they are not required to fulfill that obligation at the Vigil Mass specifically. As an encouragement to participate in this, the most solemn liturgy of Church's year, this plenary indulgence is available under the usual

---

134. The only restriction here would be that of generally limiting the acquisition of plenary indulgences to one per day. Enchiridion 1999, Norm 18 § 1.

135. *Professio Fidei et actus virtutum theologalium.* Enchiridion 1999, conc. 28 § 1; Enchiridion 1986, conc. 70. See also Raccolta, no. 679 which offered a one-sentence example of such a profession.

136. See also Raccolta, no. 44, wherein this same indulgence was offered to those faithful who joined with the celebrant in praying the Creed at Mass.

conditions even to those who are satisfying their obligation of Mass attendance by going to the Easter Vigil.

Every Catholic should know the date of his or her baptism.[137] On that day, renewing one's profession of faith, whether alone or, even better, with others, and using any approved formula, is enriched with a plenary indulgence under the usual conditions.[138]

Special visit to a cemetery.[139] Besides the partial indulgence offered for a visit to a cemetery discussed earlier, a plenary indulgence, under the usual conditions and applicable only to the souls in Purgatory, is available to the faithful who devoutly visit a cemetery any time from November 1–8 (inclusive) and who offer any prayers (even mental ones) for the dead.[140] Those for whom one might wish to apply the indulgence obtained need not be buried in the cemetery visited.

Diocesan Synod.[141] Diocesan synods (originally, assemblies of the bishop and his leading clergy) date far back in Church history, but over the centuries they fell into disuse. Only in more recent decades have diocesan synods begun to make their reappearance. Today, under the headship of the bishop, a diocesan synod calls together clergy, religious, and laity in order to examine questions affecting the good of the diocese.[142]

A plenary indulgence is offered under the usual conditions to those faithful who, during the time of a diocesan synod, devoutly visit

---

137. Most people can learn their baptismal date by sending a letter to the parish where they were baptized that gives their name, their parents' names, and the approximate date of the baptism. One should include one's telephone number, and enclose a self-addressed postcard or envelope. A donation is not required, but a check for a few dollars is a nice gesture.

138. Formulas that would certainly be acceptable here would include the Apostles' Creed, the Nicene Creed, and the Renewal of Baptismal Vows from the Easter Vigil. Slightly longer, but well worth the effort, is the "Credo of the People of God," composed by Pope Paul VI and published on 30 June 1968. The actual profession of faith begins a dozen or so paragraphs into the document.

139. *Pro fidelibus defunctis.* Enchiridion 1999, conc. 29 § 1, 1°; Enchiridion 1986, conc. 13. See also Raccolta, no. 592. Note that all indulgences available under this grant may be applied only to the poor souls in Purgatory.

140. One might want to use the special prayers for visiting a cemetery that are provided in the *Book of Blessings*, Chapter 57; *Shorter Book of Blessings*, Chapter 35. November 1 is the Solemnity of All Saints and the week following, of course, is its octave.

141. Enchiridion 1999, conc. 31; Enchiridion 1986, conc. 58. The modern norms on the conduct of diocesan synods are contained in 1983 CIC 460–468. See also CCC 887, 911.

142. See 1983 CIC 460–468.

the church in which the synod is being held and pray there an *Our Father* and a *Creed*. This indulgence may be obtained by an individual only once during a synod. There is no requirement that one be a participant in the synod or even a resident of the diocese in which the synod is being held. If the synod is not being held in a church (and most are not held in churches anymore), it would be for the diocesan bishop to designate a church where the indulgence could be obtained. This would likely be the diocesan cathedral, but there is no requirement on the point.

Pastoral Visits.[143] Most parishes look forward to the visitation of their bishop.[144] It is a time of special closeness and unity between bishop and people, and it is usually marked by liturgical celebrations, meetings with parish groups, and so on. To encourage the faithful to take advantage of these opportunities to get to know their bishop better and to express their unity in faith with him, a plenary indulgence is offered under the usual conditions to all those who participate in a sacred function (e.g., Mass) held during the bishop's visitation.

Special Prayers of Supplication and Gratitude on Certain Days.[145] Two renowned prayers, the *Veni, Creator* (*Come, Creator*) and the *Te Deum* (*You God*) are the subject of plenary indulgences under the usual conditions if offered on certain days of the year: the *Veni Creator* when offered either on the first day of the year to implore the help of God in the coming year or on the Feast of Pentecost; the *Te Deum* when offered on the last day of the year in thanksgiving for the benefit God showers on his people.[146]

---

143. *Visitatio pastoralis.* Enchiridion 1999, conc. 32; Enchiridion 1986, conc. 69.

144. Canon Law generally requires that such episcopal visitations be made to a parish at least every five years. (See 1983 CIC 396.) Under certain circumstances, this visitation might be made by someone other than the diocesan bishop (usually an episcopal vicar, who may or may not be a bishop himself); in such cases, *favores ampliari*, the indulgence attached to the visitation would still apply. This indulgence would also seem to apply to pastoral visits made to non-parochial groups, provided that the group was considered a pastoral unit such as a campus ministry association or other established chaplaincy.

145. *Preces supplicationis et gratiarum actionis.* Enchiridion 1999, conc. 26 § 1; Enchiridion 1986, conc. 60 (*Te Deum*) and 61 (*Veni, Creator*). See also Raccolta, no. 283 (*Veni, Creator*), no. 681 (*Veni, Creator*), and no. 685 (general prayers of thanksgiving at year's end and at New Year's.)

146. If these prayers are offered on other days, they are partially indulgenced (Enchiridion 1999, conc. 26 § 2), though this fact would have been apparent by the normal operation of the rules on indulgence without it having been explicated in the norms. That said, it is worth

Pilgrimages and Visits to Sacred Places, Near and Far.[147] One of the great implications of Mystery of the Incarnation is that, by becoming man and being born at a certain time in a certain place, Christ made things like time and place important for us. Lifting these aspects of our human nature to a higher level, he gave them a role in our salvation. Almost from the first formal use of the term indulgence, travel (say to a distant battleground or to a holy shrine) has been linked to the gift of indulgences.[148] Journeys, even in modern times, are not undertaken without some efforts (and sometimes with some risk) and, in any case, they are a fitting model of our time on this earth as a life-long pilgrimage toward our heavenly home. The Church today rewards our efforts to bring ourselves closer to holy places, near and far, with indulgences of different types.[149] Some of these indulgences are tied, moreover, not simply to place but also to time, and they vary in the benefit derived, depending on *when* holy visits to these sites are made. All of this can be complicated.

A plenary indulgence under the usual conditions is offered to the faithful upon visiting the following sites, and there praying an *Our Father* and a *Creed*.

1. A visit to any of the four Papal Basilicas in Rome,[150] namely, St. Peter's in the Vatican, St. John Lateran, St. Paul's Outside the Walls, and St. Mary Major. The visit can be made at any time, but the one seeking the plenary indulgence must either be part of a pilgrimage group, or be making the visit as sign of filial submission to the Roman Pontiff.

---

considering that the terms "first day of the year" and "last day of the year" seem open to interpretation, at least in so far as the State's new year (January 1) and last day of the year (December 31) do not coincide with the Church's new year (First Sunday of Advent) and last day of the year (Saturday before the First Sunday of Advent). Given that so many important things in ecclesiastical life are geared to the *liturgical* year, and not to the civil calendar, I suggest that, *favores ampliari*, those marking the liturgical year with these prayers qualify for the plenary indulgences presented here in recognition of their efforts to think with the Church.

147. See generally, *Visitationes locorum sacrorum*. Enchiridion 1999, conc. 33.

148. Hagedorn, pp. 33–37; de Angelis, nos. 20–22. See generally Raccolta, nos. 773–781.

149. Circumstances may also suggest using at the outset of such journeys the "Blessing of Pilgrims or the Blessing of Travelers" contained in the *Book of Blessings*, Chaps. 8–9 *Shorter Book of Blessings*, Chaps. 7–8.

150. *Visitationes locorum sacrorum*. Enchiridion 1999, conc. 33 § 1, 1°; Enchiridion 1986, conc. 11 (wherein the plenary indulgence was limited to visits made on the basilica's titular feast, Sundays and holy days of obligation, and any other single day in a year chosen by the visitor).

2. A visit to a minor basilica[151] on any of the following days: (a) the Feast of the Apostles Peter and Paul (June 29); (b) the titular feast of the basilica visited; (c) August 2, in honor of the "Portiuncula" indulgence; or (d) on any other single day of the year chosen by the Christian faithful visitor.

3. A visit to a cathedral church[152] on any of the following days: (a) the Feast of the Apostles Peter and Paul (June 29); (b) the titular feast of the cathedral visited; (c) on the day on which the Feast of the Chair of Peter is celebrated (usually February 22); (d) on the dedication of the Arch-basilica of the Most Holy Savior (usually November 9); or (e) August 2, in honor of the "Portiuncula" indulgence.

4. A visit to an international, national, or diocesan shrine established by competent authority[153] on any of the following days: (a) on the titular feast of the shrine; (b) on any single day in the year chosen by the visitor; (c) as often one participates in a group pilgrimage to the site.

5. A visit to a parochial church[154] on either of the following days: (a) on the titular feast of the church; or, (b) August 2, in honor of the "Portiuncula" indulgence.

6. A visit to a church or altar on the day of its dedication.[155] This indulgence applies only to the day of dedication, and not to their anniversaries.[156]

7. A visit to a church or oratory of an institute or society of consecrated life,[157] on a day dedicated to its founder. This indulgence would

---

151. *Visitationes locorum sacroum* Enchiridion 1999, conc. 33 § 1, 2°.

152. *Visitationes locorum sacrorum* Enchiridion 1999, conc. 33 § 1, 3°; Enchiridion 1986, conc. 65 (wherein the plenary indulgence in regard to cathedrals was not made available on the Feast of the Apostles Peter and Paul, the Feast of the Chair of Peter, or on the dedication of the Arch-basilica of the Most Holy Savior). For pre-conciliar treatment of the Portiuncula indulgence, see Raccolta no. 698.

153. *Visitationes locorum sacrorum* Enchiridion 1999, conc. 33 § 1, 4°.

154. *Visitationes locorum sacrorum* Enchiridion 1999, conc. 33 § 1, 5°; Enchiridion 1986, conc. 65. Although a parish usually bears the same name as the church, in case of a difference between the parish name and the church (as might happen, say, as a result of parish consolidations), it would be the name of the church that controls for purposes of this indulgence.

155. *Visitationes locorum sacrorum* Enchiridion 1999, conc. 33 § 1, 5°; Enchiridion 1986, conc. 66.

156. If a church (1983 CIC 1212, 1217–1218) or altar (1983 CIC 1212, 1237–1238) were to be re-dedicated, *favores ampliari*, the indulgence would be available again at that time.

157. *Visitationes locorum sacrorum* Enchiridion 1999, conc. 33 § 1, 7°; Enchiridion 1986, conc. 68 (wherein the indulgence was limited only to churches or oratories of *religious* instead of the broader category of "institutes of consecrated life").

not apply in the case of a parish "entrusted" to religious, even if the parish or church bears the name of saint related to the institute of consecrated life.

Visiting a Stational Church.[158] A plenary indulgence under the usual conditions is offered to those faithful who visit a "Stational Church" on its stational day and participate in sacred services there.[159] The history of "station churches" goes back at least fifteen centuries. These churches served as special gathering places for Christians making pilgrimages or when engaging in special liturgical or devotional practices.

All stational churches—the most famous being Santa Sabina, where the pope customarily distributes ashes on Ash Wednesday—are located in Rome and instructions on making use of this indulgence while in Rome are plentiful. Visits to these churches on other days of the year satisfy for partial indulgences.

Visit to the Ancient Cemeteries and Catacombs.[160] A partial indulgence is offered to those faithful who make a devout visit to any ancient Christian cemetery or catacomb. The most common examples of such catacombs are found in Rome, of course, but the tenor of the grants makes the indulgence applicable to all cemeteries of ancient Christians anywhere in the world. As a rule, early Christian cemeteries may be reckoned as those dating to the first three or four centuries of the Church.[161] Other things being equal, a visit to an ancient cemetery seems a more noble act, given the extra effort required to visit them (for they are fewer in number), and because of their greater closeness to the days of severe sufferings that the Church underwent in those early centuries.

---

158. *Visitationes locorum sacrorum* Enchiridion 1999, conc. 33 § 2; Enchiridion 1986, conc. 56 (wherein the plenary indulgence was limited to those who took part in "morning or evening services" conducted therein).

159. Thus, Morning Prayer or Evening Prayer from the Liturgy of the Hours would satisfy here, as would, of course, participation in Mass (not necessarily requiring reception of the Eucharist, though that would be appropriate given the usual requirements for plenary indulgences). Other devotional events such as adoration of the Eucharist, the Stations of the Cross, or recitation of the Rosary would probably not qualify toward this plenary indulgence, as they are devotional, not liturgical, in character. This particular grant does not reiterate the requirement of offering an *Our Father* and a *Creed* at the church (as is required by Enchiridion 1999, Norm 19), but the safer course is to include them.

160. *Visitationes locorum sacrorum.* Enchiridion 1999, conc. 33 § 3; Enchiridion 1986, conc. 14.

161. If one is not sure of the age of the cemetery in question, one may still regard it as a visit to a cemetery, indulgenced under Enchiridion 1999, conc. 29 § 2, 1°.

Divine Mercy Sunday.[162] A plenary indulgence under the usual conditions is offered on the first Sunday after Easter. It is unusual in several respects.

First, although the indulgence has nothing to do with a church or oratory, a visit to such a site is a part of the requirement for the indulgence.[163] Second, the options of either taking part in public devotions to the Divine Mercy or of making a visit to the Blessed Sacrament (exposed or reserved) and reciting an *Our Father*, a *Creed*, and a pious invocation to the Merciful Lord are equally offered. Third, alternative methods of satisfying the requirements for the indulgence are offered even beyond these two options, namely, those who are legitimately prevented from going to a church at that time may resolve to satisfy the usual conditions as soon as possible and recite an *Our Father*, a *Creed*, and a pious invocation to the Merciful Lord before an image of the Divine Mercy, and finally, for those for whom even this is impossible, they may unite themselves by spiritual intention with those performing the prescribed actions on Divine Mercy Sunday, offer an invocation to the Merciful Jesus, and resolve to complete the three usual conditions for a plenary indulgence as soon as possible. It would be difficult to imagine how the satisfaction of the requirements of this plenary indulgence could have been more accommodated to the situations of more people than has already occurred.

Prayers of the Eastern Churches.[164] All indulgences currently authorized by the Church are available to all the faithful, whether of Western or Eastern tradition.[165] Recognizing, though, that many prayers are more popular in one tradition while less known in the other, special effort is made to include Eastern prayers in the lists of those indulgenced by the Church, both to facilitate the Eastern faith-

---

162. This indulgence was established on June 29, 2002, thus after the Enchiridion 1999 was published. It is recorded in the 2004 printing of the *Enchiridion Indulgentiarum*, pp. 84–89. Priests in pastoral ministry are specifically directed to make known this new indulgence.

163. This seems reminiscent of the times when a visit to a church or oratory was considered a "usual condition" of most plenary indulgences. See Hagedorn, pp. 128–129 and de Angelis, nos. 82–84.

164. *Preces Orientalium Ecclesiarum*. Enchiridion 1999, conc. 23; Enchiridion 1986, conc. 48.

165. This was recognized even before the 1917 Code went into effect. See Hagedorn, p. 86; de Angelis, nos. 136–138.

ful in making use of indulgences, and to help introduce Western Christians to the spiritual traditions of the Eastern Churches.

Listed in the first place for a plenary indulgence under the usual conditions is the *Akathistos*, a long hymn/office in honor of Mary the Mother of God (which need not be prayed in its entirety), or alternatively, the *Paraclisis*, also Marian and intercessory in character. For either of these, Patriarchs are permitted to substitute other Marian devotional prayers according to their judgment.

For partial indulgence, the following prayers are listed: *Oratio pro gratiarum actione* (Armenian); *Oratio vespertina, Oratio pro defunctis* (Byzantine); *Oratio Sanctuarii, Oratio "Lakhu Mara" seu "Ad te Domine"* (Chaldean); *Oratio ad thurificationem, Oratio ad glorificandam Dei Matrem Mariam* (Coptic); *Oratio pro remissione peccatorum*, and *Oratio pro adipiscenda sequela Christi* (Ethiopian); *Oratio pro Ecclesia*, and *Oratio post expletam Liturgiam* (Maronite); *Intercessiones pro defunctis ex Liturgia S. Iacobi* (Syro-Antiochene).

Plenary Indulgence at the Time of Death.[166] This is one of the most famous indulgences ever offered, and is one with several unusual features.[167]

Ordinary circumstances. No priest or bishop who administers the sacraments to a member of the Christian faithful in danger of death should fail to extend to them the apostolic blessing, to which a plenary indulgence is attached.[168] Any of the sacraments normally offered to Catholics in danger of death (Anointing, Confession, and the Eucharist) can serve as the normal occasion for the apostolic blessing, though, *favores ampliari*, the actual administration of sacrament at that same time would seem not to be required.

Very importantly, the other usual conditions for obtaining a plenary indulgence are dispensed in danger-of-death cases, provided that the individual seeking the indulgence was in the habit of regular

---

166. *In articulo mortis.* Enchiridion 1999, conc. 12; Enchiridion 1986, conc. 28.

167. The description of this indulgence includes an unusual but strong recommendation that it be explained to the faithful in catechisms, etc. Enchiridion 1999, conc. 12 § 5.

168. That imparting the apostolic blessing to the dying and those in danger of death is an entrusted function of pastors (1983 CIC 530, 3°) does not restrict the ability of any priest to confer this blessing with its plenary indulgence. See also 1983 CIC 529 § 1.

prayer.[169] The indulgence need not be consciously sought at the time of death but, although the desire for this indulgence can be imputed to Catholics who try to live the faith in an active way, it is pastorally advisable for each member of the faithful to express to God—and if possible to loved ones who might be expected to be in attendance at death—the desire to receive the sacraments and this indulgence at the proper time. The use of a cross or crucifix is recommended (there certainly is no prohibition against using other objects of devotion), and this indulgence can be obtained even if one has obtained another plenary indulgence that same day.

Extraordinary circumstances. If a priest cannot be present at the time of death, the Church still extends the plenary indulgence to Christians who are in the habit of praying regularly. In every other respect, the requirements for the acquisition of this indulgence under ordinary circumstances apply.

As a conclusion, Table 5.1 summarizes simply the two categories of indulgences.

Table 5.1   Categories of Indulgences

General Grant Indulgences (All General Grant indulgences are partial.)				Specific Grant Indulgences (Most Specific Grant indulgences are partial, but some are, or can become, plenary.			
I	II	III	IV	I	II	III	IV
Patient Acceptance	Service to Others	Self Denial	Public Witness	Shorter Prayers	Longer Prayers	Specific Actions	Special Occasions

While this completes our review of the indulgences now in force, from time to time special indulgences might be declared for limited times or to mark special events. Often these announcements contain little by way of explanation of how indulgences operate, but it is clear that the rules explained in this book apply also to these special indulgences.

---

169. What was widely assumed to have been an additional requirement for this indulgence, namely, specifically invoking the name of Jesus (see Raccolta, *passim*), has clearly not been carried into the discipline of indulgences.

Epilogue: Concluding Thoughts

Are indulgences the most important thing to pursue in the Christian life? Hardly. Any number of more fundamental goals or methods demand a Christian's attention before pursuing indulgences. "[A]nd you shall love the LORD your God with all your heart, with all your soul, with all your might,"[1] and "You shall love your neighbor as yourself,"[2] or even "Whoever would love life and see good days . . . must turn from evil and do good"[3] spring to mind as more important. Moreover, there are the sacraments and the sacramentals, preeminently the liturgy, and especially the Eucharist,[4] as the first means given by Christ to pursue union with him in this life. Indeed, Pope Paul VI observed:

> Therefore Holy Mother Church, supported by these truths, while again recommending to the faithful the practice of indulgences as something very dear to the Christian people during the course of many centuries and in our days as well—this is proven by experience—does not in any way intend to diminish the value of other means of sanctification and purification, first and foremost among which are the Sacrifice of the Mass and the Sacraments, particularly the Sacrament of Penance. Nor does it diminish the importance of those abundant aids which are called sacramentals or of the works of piety, penitence, and charity. All these aids have this in common, that they bring about sanctification and purification all the more efficaciously, the more closely the faithful are united with Christ the Head and the Body of the Church by charity.[5]

But for those who already make ample use of the ordinary means of sanctification, who strive to live a liturgically active faith, and who seek without guile or reluctance to make humble use of every means that God offers to move closer to him, for such people, indulgences can make an important contribution to the spiritual life.

1. Deuteronomy 6:5.

2. Mark 12:30–31.

3. 1 Peter 3:11; 1 Thessalonians 5:21.

4. For the liturgy, especially the Eucharist, as the "source and summit" of the Christian life, see, *Lumen gentium* 11, *Sacrosanctum Concilium* 10.

5. Doctrina, 11. See also Enchiridion 1999, Introduction, no. 3.

Remember, God made us to be forever with him in paradise. Everything God did in making indulgences available to us, he did in order to bring us ever closer to him in this life and to prepare our place with him in the next. As we stated at the outset of this book, neither God nor his Church forces the faithful to make use of indulgences, but for too long it seems, too many Christians have lost sight of the benefit of indulgences. However, as we have seen, it is never too late to accept the gift of indulgences and to make them a part of one's vibrant life in the Lord.

Selected Bibliography

1. Official Latin sources on indulgences

[1983] Codex Iuris Canonici, auctoritate Ioannis Pauli PP. II promulgatus (Roma: Libreria Editrice Vaticana, 1983), cc. 992–997. See also [1917] *Codex Iuris Canonici, Pii X Pontificis Maximi, iussu digestus; Benedicti Papae XV, auctoritate promulgatus* (Typis Polyglottis Vaticanis, 1918), cc. 911–936.

Paul VI, apostolic constitution, *Indulgentiarum doctrina*, 1 January 1967, *Acta Apostolicae Sedis* 59 (1967), pp. 5–24.

Sacra Paenitentiaria Apostolica, decretum Novum "Enchiridion Indulgentiarum" editur, 29 June 1968, *Acta Apostolicae Sedis* 60 (1968), pp. 413–419.

Catechismus Catholicae Ecclesiae, 2d ed., (Vatican City: Libreria Editrice Vaticana, 1997), nos. 1471–1479.

2. Selected post-*Doctrina* discussions of indulgences

All major commentaries on the 1983 Code contain useful discussions of indulgences. Some of the more accessible are:

John McAreavey, "Commentary on 1983 CIC 992–997," in G. Sheehy, et al., eds., *The Canon Law: Letter and Spirit* (Collegeville, MN: Liturgical Press, 1995), pp. 539-541.

Frederick McManus, "Commentary on 1983 CIC 992–997," in J. Beal, et al., eds., *New Commentary on the Code of Canon Law* (Mahwah, NJ: Paulist, 2000), pp. 1172–1178; see also his virtually identical commentary in J. Coriden, et al., eds., *The Code of Canon Law: a Text and Commentary* (Mahwah, NJ: Paulist, 1985) pp. 697–701.

Other treatments include:

John Hardon, *The Catholic Catechism* (New York: Doubleday, 1975) pp. 560–570. This well-known work is a good catechetical explanation of modern indulgences.

P. Palmer & G. Tavard, "Indulgences," New *Catholic Encyclopedia*, 2d ed., (Farmington Hills, MI: Thomson Gale, 2003) vol. 7, pp. 436–440.

James Akin, "Indulgences", *The Salvation Controversy*, (El Cajon, CA: Catholic Answers, 2001) pp. 52–71. This is a clear and helpful, apologetics-oriented examination.

3. Selected pre-*Doctrina* studies of indulgences

All major commentaries on the 1917 Code, too many to list here, contain useful discussions of indulgences.

Other treatments include:

Seraphinus de Angelis, *De Indulgentiis: Tractatus quoad earum naturam and usum* [Treatise on the nature and use of indulgences] 2d ed. (Vatican City: Libreria Editrice Vaticana, 1947/1950) [herein, de Angelis, *Indulgences*]. A clearly presented and highly reliable explanation of the discipline of indulgences as it existed just before the Second Vatican Council. All translations herein mine.

P. Palmer, "Indulgences", *The New Catholic Encyclopedia*, vol. 7 (New York: McGraw Hill, 1966), pp. 482–484; O. Boenki, "Indulgences, Apostolic," ibid., pp. 484–485, and J. Markham, "Indulgences, Canon Law of," ibid., pp. 485–486. These contributions are all well done.

W. H. Kent, "Indulgences" and "Indulgences, Apostolic," *The Catholic Encyclopedia*, vol. VII (New York: Robert Appleton, 1910) pp. 783–789. This classic text contains excellent short studies, with valuable pre-twenthieth century bibliographies. Available on line at www.newadvent.org.

St. Thomas Aquinas, *Summa Theologica*, Supplement, part III, Question 25 "Of Indulgences," Blackfriars' translation, (New York: Benziger Brothers, 1948) pp. 2651–2659. This great work is of course a major milestone in the development of Church teaching on indulgences.

Name and Subject Index

Precept 57, 91
  Lord's precept 78. See also Our Father.
  Precepts of the Church 35
Presumption 34, 44
Profession of Faith 61, 73, 86, 88, 95–96
Psalms 75
Punishment 2, 3, 4, 5, 9, 13, 20, 21,
  22–26, 28, 29, 30, 31, 32, 33, 42,
  46, 48, 49, 50, 51, 52, 53, 54. See
  also Liability (of Punishment).
Punishment, eternal 3, 21, 22, 25, 32, 43
Punishment, temporal or temporary 2,
  3, 4, 9, 25, 30, 32, 36
Purgatory 1, 2, 3, 10, 11, 13, 21, 22, 25,
  31, 47, 49, 50, 73, 78, 79, 88, 96

Raccolta 8, 9, 15, 41, 61, 62, 64, 67, 70,
  71, 72, 73, 74, 75, 76, 77, 78, 79,
  80, 81, 82, 83, 84, 87, 88, 89, 91,
  92, 93, 94, 95, 96, 97, 98, 99, 103
Recordings or broadcasts 88, 89, 90, 92, 93
Regina caeli: see Angelus or Regina caeli
Regulae Iuris (Boniface VIII) 44
Religious Ends, promotion of 90–91
Remission of punishment for sin 2, 30,
  31, 32, 36, 48, 50, 52
Repentance 5, 10, 52
Retreat 84
Roman Law 5
Rosary (or Marian Rosary) 33, 41, 42,
  44, 59, 60, 69, 71, 75–76, 78, 93,
  100, 102
  Rosary (other kinds) 76
  Rosary (papal) 93

Sacred Heart, reparation to viii, 75, 77,
  78, 79, 80
Sacred Scripture viii, 4, 5, 71, 80, 86
  Indulgence for reading Scripture 66,
  80, 84, 88
Sacrilege 28, 35, 39
Saints, merits of 7, 10, 11, 30, 45–46,
  48, 66
Salve Regina 59, 71
Satispassion 22
Sayers, Dorothy 3
Schism 35
Scrupulosity 22, 34, 44, 76
Sign of the Cross 41, 69, 87–88

Sin 18–29
Sin, attachment to: see Attachment
  to sin.
Sin, effects of 22–25
Sin, grave or mortal 2, 19, 20, 21, 22,
  23, 24, 25, 26, 27, 28, 29, 32, 34,
  35, 36, 42, 43
Sin, Original 19, 22, 26, 27, 29
Sin, venial or light or daily 9, 16, 20,
  21, 22, 23, 24, 25, 26, 27, 28, 32,
  36, 42, 43
Soteriology 1, 18
Spiritual Communion 39, 81, 82
Spiritual exercises 83, 84
Stational Church 100
Stations of the Cross 41, 84–86, 100
Suarez, Francisco 8
Suffrage for the dead 6, 10, 48, 49, 74, 80
Supplication 70, 73, 97
Synod, diocesan 56, 57, 96–97

Tertullian 5
Thanksgiving 70, 73, 82, 83, 97
Theological virtues (Acts of Faith,
  Hope, and Charity) 77, 78
Time of Death, Indulgence at 102–103
Time periods (old system for measuring
  indulgences) 9, 50
Toledo, Council of 5
Trafficking in indulgences 8, 70
Translation 60, 69, 74
Treasury of the Church (or, of Merits)
  2, 7, 9, 19, 30, 44, 45–46, 51, 53
Trent, Council of 1, 8, 9, 16, 65

Unigenitus Dei Filius, (Clement VI) 7, 8
Urban II, Pope 6

Vatican II 2, 11, 12, 15, 33, 78, 79
  cons. Lumen gentium 2, 4, 33, 79
Work, general performance of 9, 13, 16,
  20, 34, 35, 37–41, 42, 44, 48, 49,
  50, 52, 53, 57, 58, 59, 64, 66, 67,
  76, 84, 91, 92, 94, 101
Works, to be performed personally 8,
  13, 15, 16, 31, 35, 38, 39, 40, 41,
  42, 43, 48, 57–60, 61, 67, 104
World Alliance of Reformed Churches vi
Wyclif 7

Numerical Reference Index

c. 276	58	c. 1006	28
c. 368	54	c. 1007	28
c. 369	54	c. 1170	33
c. 370	54	c. 1183	33
c. 371	54	c. 1212	99
c. 383	70	c. 1214	39
c. 396	97	c. 1215	39
c. 435	55	c. 1216	39
c. 438	55	c. 1217	39, 99
c. 460	96	c. 1218	39, 99
c. 461	96	c. 1219	39
c. 462	96	c. 1220	39
c. 463	96	c. 1221	39
c. 464	96	c. 1222	39
c. 465	96	c. 1223	39
c. 466	96	c. 1224	39
c. 467	96	c. 1225	39
c. 468	96	c. 1226	39
c. 529	102	c. 1227	39
c. 530	102	c. 1228	39
c. 663	58	c. 1229	39
c. 755	70	c. 1230	56
c. 766	87	c. 1231	56
c. 827	80	c. 1232	56
c. 837	60	c. 1233	56
c. 844	33, 34	c. 1234	56
c. 845	21, 33	c. 1237	99
c. 846	60	c. 1238	99
c. 849	33	c. 1247	57, 82
c. 857	56	c. 1248	82
c. 860	56	c. 1249	66
c. 897	82	c. 1250	66, 92
c. 916	28, 39	c. 1251	66, 92
c. 917	40	c. 1252	66
c. 919	82	c. 1253	66
c. 920	40, 82	c. 1311	35
c. 934	57	c. 1323	35
c. 959	23	c. 1324	35
c. 960	28	c. 1331	35
c. 961	28	c. 1332	35
c. 962	28	c. 1347	35
c. 963	28, 29	c. 1364	35
c. 982	24	c. 1367	35
c. 988	27	c. 1370	35
c. 992	18, 19, 30, 32	c. 1378	35
c. 993	18	c. 1382	35
c. 994	18, 33, 74	c. 1388	35
c. 995	18, 45	c. 1390	24
c. 996	18, 33	c. 1398	35
c. 997	18		

About the Liturgical Institute

The Liturgical Institute, founded in 2000 by His Eminence Francis Cardinal George of Chicago, offers a variety of options for education in Liturgical Studies. A unified, rites-based core curriculum constitutes the foundation of the program, providing integrated and balanced studies toward the advancement of the renewal promoted by the Second Vatican Council. The musical, artistic, and architectural dimensions of worship are given particular emphasis in the curriculum. Institute students are encouraged to participate in its "liturgical heart" of daily Mass and Morning and Evening Prayer. The academic program of the Institute serves a diverse, international student population—laity, religious, and clergy—who are preparing for service in parishes, dioceses, and religious communities. Personalized mentoring is provided in view of each student's ministerial and professional goals. The Institute is housed on the campus of the University of St. Mary of the Lake/Mundelein Seminary, which offers the largest priestly formation program in the United States and is the center of the permanent diaconate and lay ministry training programs of the Archdiocese of Chicago. In addition, the University has the distinction of being the first chartered institution of higher learning in Chicago (1844), and one of only seven pontifical faculties in North America.

For more information about the Liturgical Institute and its programs, contact: usml.edu/liturgicalinstitute. Phone: 847-837-4542. E-mail: litinst@usml.edu.

Msgr. Reynold Hillenbrand
1904-1979

Monsignor Reynold Hillenbrand, ordained a priest
by Cardinal George Mundelein in 1929, was Rector
of St. Mary of the Lake Seminary from 1936 to 1944.

He was a leading figure in the liturgical and social
action movement in the United States during the
1930s and worked to promote active, intelligent,
and informed participation in the Church's liturgy.

He believed that a reconstruction of society would
occur as a result of the renewal of the Christian
spirit, whose source and center is the liturgy.

Hillenbrand taught that, since the ultimate purpose
of Catholic action is to Christianize society, the
renewal of the liturgy must undoubtedly play the
key role in achieving this goal.

Hillenbrand Books strives to reflect the spirit of
Monsignor Reynold Hillenbrand's pioneering work
by making available innovative and scholarly
resources that advance the liturgical and sacramental
life of the Church.

About the Author

Dr. Edward Peters, one of the most widely-known lay canon lawyers in North America, joined the graduate faculty at Sacred Heart Major Seminary in 2005 with his appointment to the Edmund Cardinal Szoka Chair. Dr. Peters holds a JD degree from University of Missouri at Columbia. He also holds a JCL and JCD in Canon Law from the Catholic University of America in Washington, D.C. He has written for a wide variety of religious and secular publications. He appears frequently in Catholic and secular media to explain the interplay between Church law and life.

He has published *1917 Pio-Benedictine Code of Canon Law in English Translation* (2001), *Annulments and the Catholic Church* (2004), and his textual history of the 1983 Code, *Incrementa in Progressu 1983 Codicis Iuris Canonici* (2005). Peters maintains a prominent educational Web site dedicated to ecclesiastical law, www.Canonlaw.info.